THE
GROWTH
BUSINESS

THE GROWTH BUSINESS

WORK SMARTER NOT HARDER
20% GROWTH | HALF THE TIME

CLIVE SMALLMAN PhD

DESIGN FOR GROWTH

QDA Pty Ltd t/as Design for Growth
PO Box 278
Salamander Bay
NSW 2317
Australia

www.designforgrowth.com.au

Smallman, Clive

The Growth Business: Work Smarter Not Harder. 20% Growth | Half the Time

Paperback ISBN 978-0-6451824-2-2

eBook ISBN 978-0-6451824-0-8

DISCLAIMER

Contents

The Growth Business

Every business has three essential elements: revenue and cash flow, production or service delivery costs, and work-life integration - the amount of effort that founders, owners, managers and employees put into the business, and their life outside work.

Revenue and cash flow is the lifeblood of any business. *Revenue streams* are built on the *value propositions* that the business offers different *customer segments* to solve their problems and meet their needs. Key to the offer is the communication, distribution and sales *channels* through which value propositions are delivered to customers. Also crucial are the *customer relationships* that are established and maintained with each customer segments.

The **cost structure** is the skeleton of a business. Revenue streams are delivered by performing *key activities* using *key resources* or assets. Some activities are outsourced, and some resources are externally sourced, both from *key partners*.

Together the revenue streams and cost structure with their component parts describe an organisation's **business model**. How we design the different elements and operate them in the business model environment governs whether we have a **growth business** or not.

Also central to business growth is the impact of the effort put in by the people who own, manage, and work in the organisation. There is a substantial amount of evidence that demonstrates that how well our **work and lives are integrated** determines how impactful we are at work.

Design a Growth Business

Most businesses, even some of the world's biggest, aren't deliberately designed but instead evolve out of an entrepreneurial idea, which is further tweaked over time – what I call an **organic business**. Most of us try to get by with such businesses – in Australia that's called "She'll be right", in other words whatever is wrong with the business will correct itself in time.

That's not necessarily a bad thing, and it works out for some of us. But a little design goes a long way.

In this book, we're going to explore how to deliberately design and build your best business for growth in the first five steps of our *Design for Growth* coaching model and how to design your best life in the sixth and final(-ish) step. "-ish"? In our approach you don't stop tinkering with your business or your work-life. You always be fine tuning both.

We're going to look at how to unpack your business on both the revenue and cost sides of your model. We'll look at how to identify the political, economic, social and technological trends that are driving your businesses present and future. Competitive intelligence is all about building your awareness of where your business sits in the markets and segments that you operate in. We'll then look at how you evaluate your position. Based on that evaluation we look at how you can redesign your business for growth by manipulating the building blocks that comprise your revenue streams and cost structure.

With the remodelling started, we then look at how you can best manage your personal cash, assets, and life in general to better integrate work with life.

Red Lights and the Organic Business

Over the last 30 years or so of coaching, teaching and researching business, working alongside founders, owners, leaders and managers of all sorts of businesses of all sizes, I've discovered that while some of us get by without deliberate business design, many more don't.

The Australian Bureau of Statistics reckons that 48% of new businesses fail within the first four years. The University of Technology, Sydney drills down further, finding that one in three new small businesses in Australia fail in their first year of operation, two out of four by the end of the second year, and three out of four by the fifth year. The Australian Broadcasting Corporation recently found that more than 15 % of Australian businesses of all sizes failed in the 12 months to August 2023.

These figures are broadly consistent with trends in developed economies across the several decades I've been watching them.

The sources of failure? There are many, but for me, there is a consistent trend across the evidence and in work I've done.

Often, the lack of a well-designed, continuously improved business model coupled to a poorly-managed life triggers one or more "'red lights" for "organic" businesses: the challenges of the revenue rollercoaster, cost conundrum, and burnout. Each signals a distinct yet interconnected area of concern that demands swift and strategic intervention.

RED LIGHTS AND THE ORGANIC BUSINESS

Revenue Rollercoaster

This phenomenon, characterized by erratic and unpredictable financial performance, poses a significant threat to the stability and long-term viability of a business. Without a steady and predictable flow of income, strategic planning becomes a game of chance rather than a calculated effort to foster growth. It suggests an underlying issue with the business's revenue generation model—perhaps a too narrow focus on certain products or markets, or a failure to adapt to changing customer needs and market conditions.

Cost Conundrum

When businesses face persistent issues with managing expenses—whether due to operational inefficiencies, procurement practices, or misaligned resource allocation—they find themselves trapped in a cost conundrum. This state not only diminishes profitability but also threatens the financial foundation of the enterprise. It's a clear indicator that processes need to be re-evaluated and streamlined, and that a more strategic approach to cost management is required to secure the company's financial health.

Burnout

Far from being merely a personal issue, burnout among founders, owners, leaders and employees reflects a systemic problem within the business's culture and operational model. It's often both a cause and an effect of the revenue and cost challenges, manifesting in an environment that prioritizes immediate outputs over sustainable growth. Burnout erodes productivity, innovation, and morale, jeopardizing the business's ability to compete and succeed in the long term.

Together, these "red lights" underscore the necessity for a comprehensive strategy that not only addresses each issue individually but also considers their interplay. The aim should be to establish a robust framework for revenue generation, implement efficient cost control measures, and cultivate a healthy, sustainable work environment. By doing so, businesses can navigate away from these red lights and towards a path of stability, growth, and resilience.

Design for Growth

A well-designed and executed business model – a *growth business* –is foundational to achieving **consistent cash flow**, **controlled costs**, and a properly **integrated work-life**, ultimately cultivating a growth-oriented business. At the heart of such a model lies the strategic alignment of product offerings, market needs, and operational efficiency, all orchestrated to work in harmony.

THE GROWTH BUSINESS

Consistent Cash Flow

Achieving consistent cash flow in a business model revolves around the strategic alignment of the company's offerings with market demands and ensuring these offerings are delivered through efficient, customer-focused operations. This involves a nuanced approach that extends beyond simply selling products or services; it requires creating value propositions that deeply resonate with target customers and address their evolving needs.

A customer-centric revenue strategy is the cornerstone of consistent cash flow. This involves not just understanding but anticipating customer needs and preferences, thereby securing a loyal customer base that contributes to regular, predictable revenue streams. Implementing subscription models, loyalty programs, and flexible pricing structures can enhance customer retention and stabilize income.

Diversifying revenue streams mitigates the risk associated with reliance on a single source of income. By exploring multiple channels, such as online sales, partnerships, and new market segments, businesses can create additional pathways for revenue that buffer against market fluctuations and sector-specific downturns.

Operational efficiency plays a critical role in maintaining cash flow. By optimizing processes, reducing waste, and leveraging technology for automation, businesses can lower operational costs, thereby increasing the margin between revenue and expenses. **Lean management** practices encourage continuous improvement and adaptability, ensuring that the business remains agile and responsive to changes in the market.

Integral to achieving consistent cash flow is **strategic financial planning**, which includes careful budgeting, forecasting, and cash management practices. This ensures that resources are allocated efficiently, investments are made judiciously, and there is sufficient liquidity to cover operational needs. Effective financial planning provides a roadmap for growth while safeguarding against the unpredictability of business cycles.

In essence, building consistent cash flow requires a multi-faceted strategy that integrates customer-centric revenue generation with operational efficiency and strategic financial planning. It's about creating a resilient business model that not only meets the current market demands but is also agile enough to adapt to future changes, ensuring long-term sustainability and growth.

Controlled Costs

Efficient cost control is achieved through lean operations and strategic financial planning. This requires a meticulous approach to resource allocation, where every expense is justified by its contribution to value creation. Automation and process optimization play crucial roles in reducing operational inefficiencies, minimizing waste, and maximizing productivity. A culture of continuous improvement encourages ongoing scrutiny of costs and operational practices, ensuring the business remains agile and cost-effective.

There's another important point to make here. In the context of achieving controlled costs within a well-designed business model, it's crucial to reframe the concept of costs not merely as expenses to be minimized but as strategic investments that drive growth and value creation. This perspective shifts the focus from cost-cutting to value optimization, ensuring that each dollar spent contributes directly to the company's strategic objectives and competitive advantage.

Controlled costs, underpinned by a mindset of **strategic investment**, involves allocating resources toward areas with the highest return on investment (ROI). This means investing in technology that automates and streamlines operations, reducing long-term operational costs and increasing efficiency. It also involves investing in talent and training, which can lead to innovation, improved processes, and better customer service—all of which are critical for sustainable growth. Furthermore, investments in research and development (R&D) can open new revenue streams and keep the company ahead of market trends, ensuring long-term viability.

A strategic approach to costs evaluates **spending as an investment** in the company's future. For instance, marketing and sales efforts, often seen as costs, are investments in market expansion and customer acquisition. Similarly, sustainability initiatives may require upfront costs but lead to savings through efficiency improvements and enhanced brand reputation. The key is to balance short-term cost implications with long-term growth prospects, ensuring that cost management contributes to, rather than detracts from, the overall strategic goals of the business.

Embedding the concept of **costs as an investment into the organizational culture** encourages a more thoughtful approach to spending. It prompts teams across the organization to consider the strategic impact of their cost decisions and to identify opportunities where investments can lead to greater efficiency, innovation, and customer satisfaction. This cultural shift ensures that cost control becomes a collective effort aimed at enhancing value rather than merely reducing expenses.

Viewing costs through the lens of strategic investment is a cornerstone of a well-executed business model that aims for controlled costs. This approach not only ensures financial discipline but also aligns spending with the company's growth ambitions, turning cost management into a powerful tool for value creation and competitive differentiation. By carefully selecting where and how to invest, businesses can optimize their resource allocation, driving efficiency and growth in a balanced and sustainable manner.

Work-Life Harmony

Harmonising work and life into the fabric of a growth business model, particularly from the perspective of the founder, owner, or manager, is not just beneficial but critical for the long-term health and success of the business. For entrepreneurs and business leaders, achieving this balance is a testament to their ability to lead by example, demonstrating a sustainable approach to managing both the business and personal life.

As a founder or manager, embodying the principles of work-life integration in your own life sets a **powerful example** for your team. It sends a clear message that the business values and respects the need for balance, encouraging employees to adopt similar practices. This leadership style not only enhances your own quality of life but also fosters a culture of trust, respect, and mutual support within the organization.

Effective delegation is key for business leaders striving for work-life balance. By entrusting tasks and responsibilities to capable team members, you not only empower them but also free up your own time to focus on strategic decision-making and personal rejuvenation. This **trust** in delegation reflects a confident leadership that values employee growth and autonomy, contributing to a more resilient and adaptable organization.

As the architect of your business's culture, **integrating policies that support work-life harmony** across the board reflects your commitment to a healthy work environment. This includes flexible working arrangements, wellness initiatives, and encouraging time off. Such policies not only benefit employees but also reduce burnout and turnover among your team, directly impacting the business's performance and sustainability.

Embracing technology to streamline operations and improve efficiency is especially relevant for founders and managers. Tools that automate routine tasks, facilitate remote work, and enhance communication can significantly reduce the demands on your time, allowing for greater focus on strategic growth activities and personal well-being.

Finally, maintaining work-life balance as a business leader involves **continuous self-reflection and openness to adjust your approach** as needed. This means regularly assessing your work habits, the impact of your leadership style on the business and your personal life, and making necessary adjustments to ensure that both the business and your well-being are thriving.

For business founders, owners, and managers, achieving a work-life balance is not just about personal well-being; it's a strategic business decision that influences the entire organizational culture, productivity, and ultimately, the success of the business. By prioritizing this balance, leaders not only enhance their own lives but also create a supportive, efficient, and resilient business environment that is conducive to long-term growth and success.

Implementing such a business model requires visionary leadership, a willingness to experiment and learn, and a commitment to long-term goals over short-term gains. It involves aligning the company's core competencies with market opportunities, investing in technology and people, and creating a resilient organizational culture that can adapt to challenges and seize opportunities.

In essence, a growth business model is not just about what a company does, but how it does it. It's a strategic blueprint that integrates financial performance with operational efficiency and human values, leading to sustainable growth, market leadership, and a competitive edge. By focusing on consistent cash flow, controlled costs, and integrated work-life balance, businesses can not only survive but thrive, turning potential challenges into stepping stones for success.

(Re)designing the Growth Business

Based on multiple business strategy projects with students and clients, lots of research, teaching and consulting, what I figured out is what I said earlier: "a little design goes a long way".

Designing your business model in the context of the markets you operate in brings consistent cash flow, controlled costs, and best of all an integrated work-life that you will love.

As I mentioned previously, there are six stages to designing your business *and* life for growth.

IDENTIFY YOUR BUSINESS PESTs

BUILD COMPETITIVE INTELLIGENCE

UNPACK YOUR BUSINESS

EVALUATE YOUR POSITION

CONSISTENT CASH FLOW

REVENUE ROLLERCOASTER

COST CONUNDRUM

CONTROLLED COSTS

THE GROWTH BUSINESS

BURNOUT

WORK-LIFE HARMONY

DESIGN FOR LIFE

(RE)DESIGN FOR GROWTH

THE SIX STAGES TO A GROWTH BUSINESS

In Chapter One, we'll look at how to **unpack your business** using the Business Model Canvas (BMC) (Osterwalder and Pigneur, 2010). This involves a deep dive into each of nine segments of the canvas to reveal the strategic details that underpin your business's operation. This process is not just about filling in the blanks but critically analysing and understanding the interconnections between each component. By dissecting the value proposition, you unpack what sets the business apart in addressing customer needs. Exploring customer segments and relationships unveils who the business serves and how it intends to retain them. Channels and key activities highlight the pathways through which value is delivered and the actions necessary to make it happen.

Further, examining the revenue streams and cost structure provides insight into the financial viability of the business model, revealing how the company makes money and where the major expenditures lie. Key resources and partnerships are scrutinized to understand the assets the business relies on and the external collaborations that support its operations.

Chapter Two will help you explore a much-misunderstood element of business: the political, economic, social and technological trends that affect us now and into the future. This fresh take on the classic PEST analysis enriches our understanding of the external factors shaping industries. Forgive the pun, but it's about **identifying your business PESTs**, because that's what they become if you don't take care.

THE GROWTH BUSINESS

Traditionally focusing on Political, Economic, Social, and Technological influences, today's context demands a broader lens. Incorporating Environmental and Legal considerations, the updated approach acknowledges the critical impact of sustainability and regulatory changes on business operations. This expanded analysis helps businesses navigate the complexities of modern markets, offering a more holistic view of the opportunities and challenges that lie ahead. It's a strategic tool that adapts to the evolving business landscape, ensuring companies can anticipate shifts and position themselves for success in an ever-changing environment.

You're a medium-sized business and think this isn't relevant? You might need to rethink that in this age of the Internet.

Chapter Three is all about how to **build competitive intelligence**, if from a slightly different perspective, using the idea of situation analysis that is more usually found in the world of paramilitary organisations. We use this approach to better explore industry forces and market forces.

Building competitive intelligence through personal and team situation awareness involves cultivating a keen understanding of both the internal and external environments that affect your business.

It starts with individuals developing the acuity to notice changes, trends, and patterns in the market, competitor behaviour, and customer preferences. This personal awareness, when shared within a team, transforms into a collective intelligence that can anticipate competitive moves and identify strategic opportunities.

Teams that communicate effectively and share insights can quickly adapt to market shifts, leveraging this collective awareness to make informed decisions. By fostering an environment where observation, communication, and collaboration are prioritized, businesses can develop a dynamic competitive intelligence capability that is both responsive and proactive, ensuring they stay ahead in the game.

This competitive intelligence is deployed to establish and monitor what is going on in your industry (suppliers, stakeholders, incumbent competitors, new entrants, substitute products and services). It's further used to better understand and monitor your market (segments, needs and demand, challenges, switching costs, revenue attractiveness).

In Chapter Four, you'll explore how to **evaluate your position** by crafting a strategic analysis that marries the insights from unpacking a business model with a strengths, weaknesses, opportunities and threats (SWOT) analysis. Hence, you'll dissect and understand your business's core structure (based on its business model) and its standing in the competitive landscape (i.e., competitor analysis and market analysis), based on competitive intelligence. This approach begins by delving into the business model, identifying how a company creates, delivers, and captures value—pinpointing its strengths and uncovering its weaknesses.

From here, we extend our gaze outward, incorporating a SWOT analysis to map these internal insights against the backdrop of external opportunities and threats. This includes considering the broader PEST factors and the landscape of competitive intelligence, providing a comprehensive view of the business's situation with reference to the competition and its markets.

The synthesis of this analysis involves leveraging the business's strengths to tap into identified opportunities, while simultaneously addressing weaknesses and guarding against external threats. This strategic framework is not static; it demands continuous reflection and adaptation, encouraging businesses to evolve in response to both internal developments and shifts in the external environment.

This integrated approach, focusing on the business model's components and SWOT analysis, empowers businesses to navigate their competitive landscapes with precision. It ensures that strategic decisions are informed by a deep understanding of the business's unique position and the external factors that influence its success.

Chapter five is where the magic starts to happen as you **(re)design for growth**. We adapt the Four Actions Framework, integral to *Blue Ocean Strategy* (Kim and Mauborgne, 2005, 2017), which offers a transformative approach to redesigning a business model for growth by encouraging businesses to systematically rethink their strategies. This method involves evaluating every aspect of the current business model to identify opportunities for innovation and differentiation.

The first step involves scrutinizing the existing elements of the business model to identify and eliminate aspects that are taken for granted within the industry but no longer add value to customers. This could mean phasing out outdated services, technologies, or processes that consume resources without enhancing customer satisfaction or the bottom line.

Next, the focus shifts to scaling back certain elements below the industry standard. This is about identifying areas of overdesign or excessive offerings that don't align with customer priorities, allowing the business to streamline operations, reduce costs, and focus on core value propositions.

Conversely, certain aspects of the business model are identified for enhancement above the industry norm. This involves investing in and amplifying features, services, or processes that significantly boost customer value and satisfaction, potentially allowing for premium pricing and positioning.

The final, and perhaps most critical step is to innovate by creating entirely new elements that the industry has not yet offered. This is where true differentiation occurs, as businesses introduce novel products, services, or business model components that meet unaddressed customer needs or capitalize on emerging trends.

By applying this framework, businesses embark on a strategic overhaul that not only streamlines and refines their existing operations but also propels them into new markets and customer segments. It's a pathway to not just incremental improvements but to creating new market spaces that redefine the rules of competition, driving sustainable growth and profitability through unparalleled customer value.

In Chapter 6, we look at how to **design for (your best) life**. Based on the expertise of our strategic partners at *Design a Decade*, we outline how you build wealth around a life well-integrated with your work or business. Not specifically which piece of real estate or stock to buy but how to systematically build financial and day-to-day lifestyle wealth. We explain how you can do this safely and progressively, helping you set up life before the usual retirement age while supporting you to help reduce the risk of mistakes that could bring everything down.

We explore:

- True time management for all areas of life.
- Trusted personal and professional relationships.
- Simple systems to handle income and expenditure.
- Ways to plan for all areas of life and learn enough to evaluate suggestions by others.
- Processes to maintain your energy and freshness for the journey of life.
- How to build financial wealth in a systematic, orderly and progressive way.

In the summary, we pull it all together with a plan that focuses you on your next best step. What will you do today to grow your business (and life) by design?

I've thrown in some case studies and exercises to help you get the most out of the book.

Ready? Get your boots and hat on ... it's time to ride!

1. Unpack Your Business

1.1   Introduction

In today's rapidly evolving business landscape, the ability to clearly articulate and understand the foundational elements of your business is not just an advantage; it's a necessity. Enter the Business Model Canvas (BMC), a strategic management and entrepreneurial tool that has revolutionized the way businesses conceptualize and refine their operations. Developed by Osterwalder and Pigneur (2010), the BMC offers a comprehensive yet accessible framework for mapping out the essential components of any business model. There's a copy of the canvas over the page.

At its core, the BMC is composed of nine distinct segments: Key Partnerships, Key Activities, Key Resources, Value Propositions, Customer Relationships, Channels, Customer Segments, Cost Structure, and Revenue Streams. These components serve as the building blocks of a business, each playing a crucial role in its overall operation and strategy. However, the true power of the BMC lies not merely in filling out these segments with relevant details but in critically analysing and understanding the intricate interconnections between them.

This process of deep analysis is what sets apart successful businesses from their counterparts. It involves a rigorous examination of how each component of the BMC not only operates in isolation but also interacts with and influences the others. For example, a well-defined Value Proposition impacts the kind of Customer Relationships a business seeks to build, which in turn affects the Channels through which it engages with its Customer Segments. Similarly, the Key Activities undertaken by the business are deeply intertwined with its Cost Structure and Revenue Streams, shaping the financial viability of the entire model.

Thus, the BMC is not just a tool for sketching out business ideas; it's a framework for strategic thinking and innovation. By encouraging entrepreneurs and business managers to critically assess the connections between different aspects of their business, the BMC facilitates a holistic understanding of what makes the business tick. This, in turn, enables businesses to identify areas of strength and potential vulnerabilities, paving the way for strategic adjustments that can lead to more sustainable and profitable operations.

In this chapter, we will embark on a deep dive into each of the nine segments of the Business Model Canvas. Our goal is not just to fill in the blanks but to unlock the strategic insights that underpin successful business operations. Through this process, we will explore how to leverage the BMC as a dynamic tool for continuous innovation, enabling your business to adapt and thrive in the face of changing market conditions and emerging opportunities.

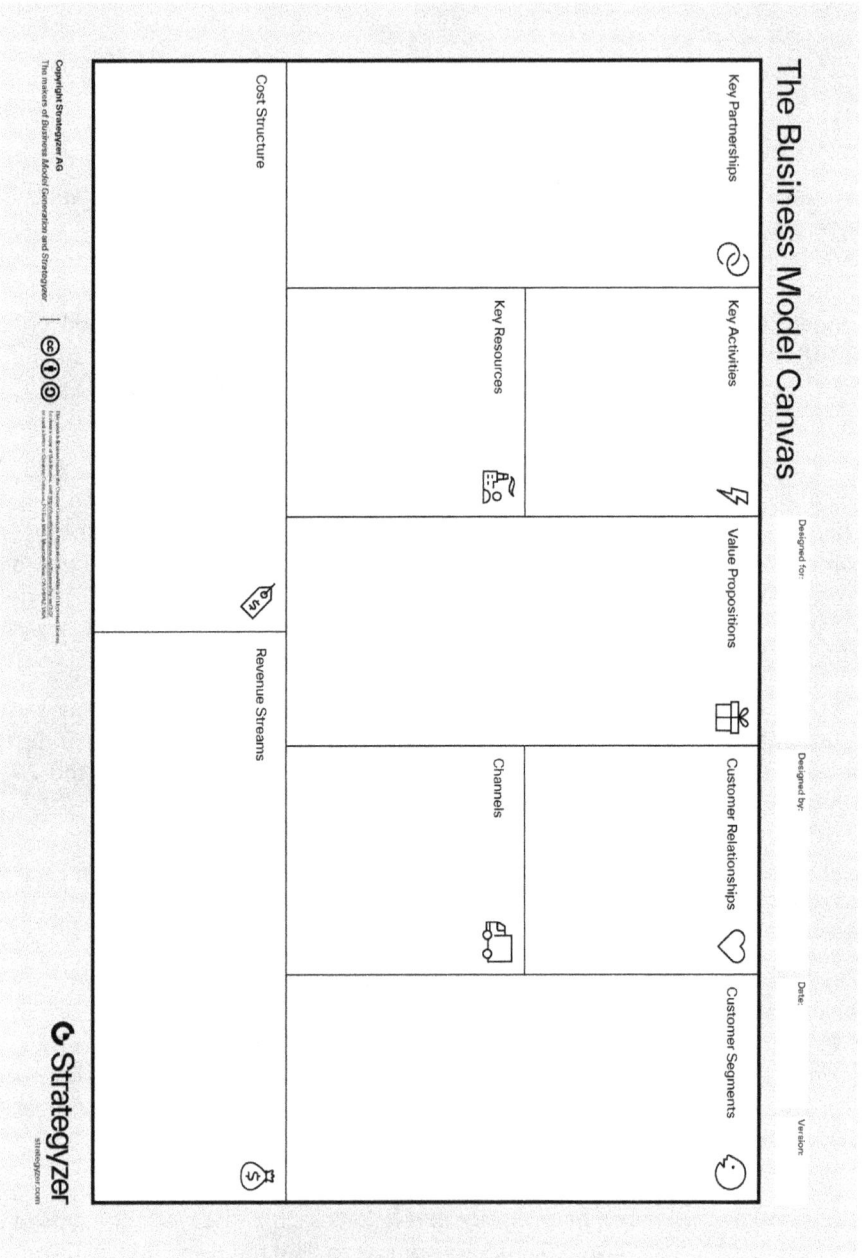

The Business Model Canvas

Key Partnerships	Key Activities	Value Propositions	Customer Relationships	Customer Segments
	Key Resources		Channels	

Cost Structure

Revenue Streams

Designed for: Designed by: Date: Version:

Strategyzer
strategyzer.com

THE BUSINESS MODEL CANVAS

1.2 Identifying Customer Segments

A fundamental step in crafting a business model that resonates with the market is identifying and understanding your Customer Segments. This segment of the Business Model Canvas focuses on who your business serves, acknowledging that different groups of customers may have varying needs, behaviors, and preferences. Successfully identifying these segments allows businesses to tailor their value propositions, marketing strategies, and overall operations to meet the specific needs of each distinct group.

1.2.1 Techniques for Identifying Customer Segments

Demographic Segmentation involves dividing the market based on demographic factors such as age, gender, income level, education, and occupation. Demographic data is relatively easy to obtain and provides a solid starting point for understanding who your customers are.

Psychographic Segmentation goes deeper by segmenting the market based on personality traits, values, attitudes, interests, and lifestyles. Psychographic segmentation helps in understanding why certain customers prefer your products or services and how they align with their personal identity or values.

Behavioural Segmentation focuses on dividing customers based on their behaviour towards products or services, including usage rate, brand loyalty, benefits sought, and purchasing patterns. Behavioural data can be particularly valuable for tailoring marketing messages and offers to fit the specific needs and preferences of different customer groups.

Geographic Segmentation, although sometimes considered part of demographic segmentation, divides the market based on location. This can include segmentation by country, region, city, or even neighbourhood. Geographic factors can significantly influence consumer preferences and purchasing habits.

1.2.2 The Role of Customer Personas in Tailoring Business Strategies

Creating detailed customer personas is a powerful way to bring your customer segments to life. A persona is a semi-fictional character that embodies the key characteristics of a significant segment of your audience. It typically includes demographic details, interests, behavioral traits, and specific needs or pain points. The process of developing customer personas involves:

- **Gathering Insights**. Collect data through customer surveys, interviews, and market research to build a comprehensive picture of your target audience.
- **Identifying Patterns**. Look for commonalities in the data that suggest distinct segments within the broader market.
- **Creating Personas**. Develop detailed profiles for each significant segment, giving them names, backgrounds, and specific characteristics that make them relatable.
- **Applying Personas**. Use these personas to guide business decisions, from product development to marketing strategies, ensuring that your offerings resonate with the specific needs and preferences of your target segments.

Personas serve as a tool for empathizing with and understanding your customers on a deeper level. They enable businesses to think from their customers' perspectives, leading to more customer-centric products, services, and marketing messages. By accurately identifying customer segments and developing detailed personas, businesses can more effectively allocate their resources, tailor their offerings, and communicate in a way that truly resonates with their intended audience, ultimately leading to higher engagement and loyalty.

1.3   The Value Proposition

At the heart of any successful business model lies its Value Proposition: the unique promise of value to be delivered to the customer. This crucial component of the Business Model Canvas (BMC) encapsulates what makes a business stand out from its competitors and pinpoints the specific benefits and solutions it offers to address customer needs. Understanding and refining your Value Proposition is a critical step in designing a business model that not only attracts but also retains customers.

1.3.1   Understanding the Value Proposition

A Value Proposition goes beyond just listing the products or services a business offers. It focuses on the unique benefits these products or services provide, such as solving a problem, fulfilling a need, or delivering a desired experience. This segment of the BMC challenges entrepreneurs to articulate why customers should choose their offering over others, essentially defining the company's identity in the market.

1.3.2   Strategies for Refining Your Value Proposition

Identify Customer Needs and Pain Points. Begin by thoroughly understanding your target customers. What are their primary needs, challenges, or desires? Conduct market research, customer interviews, and surveys to gather insights.

Analyse Competitors. Look at your competitors' value propositions. What are they offering, and how can you differentiate your offering? Aim to fill gaps in the market or provide a superior solution.

Focus on Benefits, Not Features. Emphasize the benefits your product or service brings to customers rather than just listing its features. How does it make your customers' lives better, easier, or more enjoyable?

Test and Refine. Use customer feedback, A/B testing, and market response to continuously refine your value proposition. It should be a living component of your business model that evolves based on customer needs and market dynamics.

1.3.3   Illustrative Examples of Compelling Value Propositions

Apple's value proposition has long centered around the integration of design and functionality, offering customers an unmatched user experience. This has set them apart in a crowded market of tech gadgets.

Zappos leverages exceptional customer service as a key part of its value proposition, promising not just a vast selection of shoes but also a commitment to customer satisfaction that includes easy returns and free shipping.

Tesla's value proposition focuses on innovative electric vehicles that don't compromise on performance, safety, or luxury. This has positioned Tesla as a leader in the sustainable transportation movement.

Airbnb offers a unique value proposition by providing travellers with personalized, home-like accommodations worldwide, emphasizing local experiences over traditional hotel stays.

Through these examples, it's clear that a compelling value proposition is not just about the product or service itself but about the unique way it fulfills customer needs. By meticulously defining and continuously refining this aspect of your business model, you can create a strong foundation for attracting and retaining your target audience.

1.4   Optimizing Channels

The "Channels" segment of the Business Model Canvas pertains to the various methods a business employs to communicate with its customer segments and deliver its value proposition to them. These channels are essential for marketing, sales, distribution, and after-sales support. The effectiveness of a company's channels directly influences its ability to reach its target audience, engage customers, and achieve market success. Optimizing these channels requires a strategic approach, selecting and integrating the most effective ones based on the company's goals, customer preferences, and product characteristics.

1.4.1   Analysis of Different Channels

Direct channels include in-house sales teams, company websites, and physical stores where the company interacts directly with customers. Direct channels offer high levels of control over the customer experience but can require significant investment and management.

Indirect channels involve third parties, such as retailers, distributors, and online marketplaces, to reach customers. While indirect channels can expand market reach and reduce costs, they may offer less control over the customer experience and lower profit margins.

Digital channels encompass a variety of online platforms, including social media, email marketing, SEO, and mobile apps. Digital channels are crucial for reaching and engaging modern consumers, offering scalability and detailed analytics for optimizing strategies.

Physical channels are traditional brick-and-mortar locations and physical kiosks. Despite the rise of e-commerce, physical channels remain important for offering tangible experiences, especially for products requiring physical inspection or for brands emphasizing personal service.

1.4.2   Criteria for Selecting the Most Effective Channels

Customer preferences. Choose channels based on where your target customers prefer to receive information and make purchases.

Product characteristics. Consider the nature of your product or service. High-touch or complex offerings may benefit from direct or personal channels, while standardized products can thrive in digital or indirect channels.

Cost and efficiency. Evaluate the cost-effectiveness of each channel in terms of both upfront investment and long-term operational costs, balancing these against potential reach and revenue.

Brand consistency. Ensure that the chosen channels align with your brand image and values, providing a consistent customer experience across all touchpoints.

Scalability. Consider whether the channels can scale with your business growth without compromising customer experience or operational efficiency.

1.4.3   Real-World Examples of Businesses Successfully Optimizing Their Channels

Warby Parker revolutionized the eyewear industry by combining direct online sales with a select number of physical stores. This approach allows customers to enjoy the convenience of online shopping and the tangible experience of trying on glasses in-store.

Tesla bypasses traditional dealerships, selling directly to consumers through its website and company-owned showrooms. This direct sales model enables Tesla to control the customer experience and maintain higher margins.

Nike utilizes a mix of direct-to-consumer channels, including its website and branded stores, alongside partnerships with retailers. This omnichannel strategy ensures widespread availability of its products while enhancing brand visibility and customer engagement through personalized online experiences.

Amazon has optimized its distribution channels by offering Amazon Prime, a subscription-based service providing fast, free shipping. This not only improves customer satisfaction but also encourages repeat purchases and loyalty.

These examples highlight the importance of strategically selecting and optimizing channels to effectively deliver value to customers. By aligning channel strategies with customer needs, product characteristics, and brand objectives, businesses can enhance their market reach, customer satisfaction, and competitive advantage.

1.5   Cultivating Customer Relationships

The "Customer Relationships" segment of the Business Model Canvas is integral to building a sustainable and thriving business. It focuses on the types of relationships a company establishes with its customer segments to enhance customer experience, loyalty, and retention. Recognizing and nurturing these relationships are pivotal in differentiating a business in a competitive market, ensuring not just survival but growth through repeat business and referrals.

1.5.1 Types of Customer Relationships

- **Personal assistance** involves direct human interaction between the customer and the company. This can range from in-person customer service to live chat support online. Personal assistance is valued in industries where tailored services or complex products require a human touch to guide the customer through their journey.

- In **self-service** customers independently use the services or products without direct interaction with the company. Here, the relationship is built through the ease of use, accessibility, and reliability of the product or service. Companies may provide extensive FAQs, tutorials, and community forums to support self-service models.

- A blend of self-service and personalized service, **automated services** use technology to create personalized customer experiences at scale. Examples include personalized recommendations on eCommerce sites or automated portfolio management in fintech services.

- Some companies foster customer relationships by creating **communities** around their products or services, encouraging users to connect, share experiences, and help each other. This not only enhances customer loyalty but also provides valuable feedback for the company.

- **Co-creation** invites customers to contribute to the product or service development process, creating a sense of ownership and loyalty. This can be seen in software beta testing, where users are invited to test and provide feedback on new features.

1.5.2 Significance in Customer Retention and Satisfaction

The relationship a business cultivates with its customers directly impacts retention and satisfaction. Personalized experiences make customers feel valued, increasing their loyalty and likelihood of repeat purchases. Efficient self-service options and reliable automated services can enhance satisfaction by empowering customers with convenience and speed. Communities and co-creation not only deepen the relationship but also provide invaluable insights into customer needs and preferences, enabling businesses to innovate and improve continuously.

1.5.3   Case Studies on Successful Customer Relationship Strategies

- **Amazon's personalized recommendations.** Amazon uses sophisticated algorithms to analyze shopping behavior and offer personalized product recommendations, enhancing the shopping experience and increasing sales through relevant upselling.

- **Apple's in-store Genius Bar** provides personalized tech support and repairs, creating a high-touch customer experience that reinforces brand loyalty and customer satisfaction.

- **LEGO's co-creation through LEGO ideas.** LEGO Ideas is a platform where fans can submit their own designs for new sets. Popular designs are turned into commercial products, with creators receiving recognition and a share of the profits. This approach not only engages the community but also taps into the creativity of LEGO enthusiasts, driving innovation and loyalty.

- **Fitbit Community.** Fitbit has built a strong community around its products, offering forums and groups where users can share goals, achievements, and challenges. This not only fosters a sense of belonging among users but also encourages continued use of the product.

These case studies exemplify how effectively managing customer relationships can lead to increased satisfaction, loyalty, and ultimately, business success. By understanding and strategically choosing the types of relationships to cultivate with different customer segments, businesses can create a competitive advantage that is difficult to replicate.

1.6   Unveiling Revenue Streams

The "Revenue Streams" segment of the Business Model Canvas is critical for understanding how a company generates income from its value proposition. It's about identifying all the ways a business can earn money, which sustains operations and fuels growth. For entrepreneurs and businesses looking to get off the "revenue rollercoaster," exploring and optimizing revenue streams is vital. This process involves not just diversification but also aligning revenue models with the business's value proposition and customer segments, ensuring stability and sustainability.

1.6.1   Exploration of Revenue Streams

Revenue streams can be broadly categorized into several types, each with its unique characteristics and implications for business strategy:

- **Sales Revenue**. Income generated from selling products or services. This is the most direct revenue stream and can be a one-time transaction or recurring sales.
- **Service Fees**. Earnings from providing services. This model is common in industries like consulting, where businesses charge for expertise or labor.
- **Subscription Fees**. Revenue generated by charging customers a recurring fee to access a product or service. This model provides a predictable income stream and is often used by SaaS companies, media outlets, and membership organizations.
- **Licensing Fees**. Income from allowing others to use intellectual property, such as patents, trademarks, or copyrights. This model is prevalent in technology and entertainment industries.
- **Advertising Fees**. Revenue from charging fees for advertising space on platforms owned by the business. This model is widespread in online media, social networking sites, and free apps.
- **Affiliate Revenue**. Earnings from commissions for referring customers to other businesses' products or services. Affiliate marketing is a common revenue stream for bloggers and online influencers.

1.6.2   Aligning Revenue Models with the Business's Value Proposition and Customer Segments

The choice of revenue streams should be closely aligned with the business's value proposition and the needs and preferences of its customer segments. For instance, a subscription model might appeal to customers seeking convenience and consistency, while a sales revenue model might be more appropriate for customers interested in one-time transactions. Businesses must consider factors such as customer payment preferences, the competitive landscape, and how different revenue models influence customer behaviour and loyalty.

1.6.3   Examples of Innovative Revenue Strategies

Adobe's Subscription Model. Adobe transitioned from selling perpetual software licenses to a subscription-based model with its Creative Cloud services. This shift not only stabilized revenue but also allowed for constant updates and improvements, aligning with customers' evolving needs.

Tesla's Software Updates. Tesla generates additional revenue through software updates that enhance vehicle performance and add new features. This innovative approach capitalizes on the existing customer base and demonstrates how product improvement can open new revenue streams.

Amazon Prime. Amazon's subscription service, Prime, offers free shipping, streaming, and other benefits. Prime not only generates direct subscription revenue but also increases customer loyalty and spending on Amazon's platform, showcasing the synergy between different revenue streams.

Airbnb Experiences. In addition to its core offering of accommodation rentals, Airbnb introduced "Experiences" to allow hosts to offer tours, classes, and workshops. This diversification leverages the platform's existing customer base and infrastructure to tap into new revenue streams.

For businesses seeking to escape the revenue rollercoaster, it's essential to explore and implement diverse revenue models that are synergistic with the company's core offerings and customer expectations. By innovatively aligning revenue streams with the value proposition and customer segments, companies can achieve a more stable and predictable financial performance, driving sustainable growth.

1.7   Leveraging Key Resources

The "Key Resources" segment of the Business Model Canvas focuses on the most important assets required for a business to operate successfully, deliver its value proposition, maintain customer relationships, and generate revenue. These resources can be physical, financial, intellectual, or human, and are foundational to the business's ability to compete and thrive. Effectively managing and optimizing these key resources is critical for achieving operational efficiency, fostering innovation, and sustaining competitive advantage.

1.7.1   Insight into Key Resources

Physical Resources include tangible assets such as buildings, vehicles, machinery, and inventory. These are especially critical in manufacturing, retail, and logistics businesses.

Intellectual Resources comprise patents, trademarks, copyrights, customer databases, and proprietary knowledge. Intellectual resources are vital for technology companies, creative industries, and any business with a unique innovation or brand.

Human Resources are the skills, expertise, and experiences of the company's employees. Human resources are crucial across all industries but particularly so in service-based businesses and organizations that rely heavily on personal relationships and expertise.

Financial Resources encompass cash reserves, lines of credit, and investment capital. Financial resources are necessary for all businesses to fund operations, growth, and innovation.

1.7.2   Managing and Optimizing Key Resources

Asset Utilization. Maximize the efficiency and productivity of physical resources through regular maintenance, efficient logistics, and technology integration.

Intellectual Property Protection. Safeguard intellectual resources by securing patents and trademarks. Additionally, continually innovate to stay ahead of competitors.

Talent Management. Attract, develop, and retain skilled employees through competitive compensation, professional development opportunities, and a positive work environment.

Financial Planning. Ensure financial sustainability through careful budgeting, investment in growth opportunities, and managing cash flow to handle market fluctuations.

1.7.3   Examples of Businesses Effectively Leveraging Key Resources

Apple leverages its intellectual resources, including design patents and proprietary technology, to maintain a competitive edge in the tech industry. Its brand is also a critical resource, allowing it to command premium prices.

Tesla's investment in research and development has resulted in significant intellectual property, including patents for battery technology and electric powertrains. Its Gigafactories are vital physical resources that enable large-scale production.

Google's key resources include its search algorithm and massive data centers. Human resources are also a critical asset, with the company consistently investing in top talent to drive innovation.

As a global consulting firm, **McKinsey's** primary resource is its human capital. The company invests heavily in recruiting and developing talented consultants, whose expertise and networks are critical for delivering value to clients.

By identifying, managing, and optimizing their key resources, businesses can not only ensure their operational efficiency but also innovate and adapt to changing market conditions. This strategic focus on key resources allows companies to sustain their competitive advantage, achieve long-term growth, and navigate the challenges of the business environment effectively.

1.8   Defining Key Activities

The "Key Activities" segment of the Business Model Canvas focuses on the crucial actions a company must take to ensure its business model functions effectively. These activities are essential for creating and delivering the value proposition, reaching markets, maintaining customer relationships, and ultimately generating revenue. Identifying and optimizing these key activities is vital for streamlining operations, reducing costs, and enhancing the overall efficiency and effectiveness of the business.

1.8.1   Overview of Key Activities

Key activities can vary significantly from one business model to another but generally fall into several broad categories:

- **Production**. Activities involved in the creation of a product or service. This includes manufacturing, sourcing materials, quality control, and product design.
- **Problem-solving**. Critical for service-oriented businesses, consultancy firms, and technology companies. It involves activities such as ongoing customer support, troubleshooting, and continuous product or service improvement.
- **Platform/Network Management**. Pertinent to businesses that operate on a platform model, such as social media sites, marketplace websites, or software as a service (SaaS) companies. These activities include platform maintenance, user community management, and network expansion.
- **Marketing and Sales**. Activities aimed at understanding market needs, creating customer awareness, and generating sales. This category includes advertising, promotional campaigns, and sales strategy execution.
- **Distribution**. Encompasses logistics and supply chain operations, including warehousing, inventory management, and delivery of goods and services to customers.

- **After-sales Service**. Includes customer support, maintenance services, and handling returns or complaints, which are crucial for maintaining customer satisfaction and loyalty.

1.8.2 Strategies for Streamlining Operations

- **Automation**. Identify repetitive tasks that can be automated using technology. Automation can significantly reduce the time and cost associated with these tasks, allowing staff to focus on more strategic activities.
- **Outsourcing**. For activities that are not core to your value proposition but are still necessary, consider outsourcing. This can provide access to expert skills and reduce costs compared to maintaining in-house capabilities.
- **Process Optimization**. Regularly review and optimize internal processes to eliminate inefficiencies and bottlenecks. Lean methodologies and continuous improvement practices can be effective in enhancing operational efficiency.
- **Technology Adoption**. Invest in technology solutions that can streamline operations, improve productivity, and enhance the customer experience. This includes CRM systems, project management tools, and e-commerce platforms.
- **Strategic Partnerships**. Collaborate with other businesses to share resources, knowledge, and markets. Strategic partnerships can extend your capabilities and access to new customers without the need for significant internal investment.

1.8.3 Real-World Examples

Tesla focuses on key activities like cutting-edge research and development to innovate electric vehicles and sustainable energy solutions, alongside efficient manufacturing processes to scale up production.

Airbnb concentrates on platform management, ensuring a seamless and secure experience for both hosts and guests, coupled with effective digital marketing strategies to grow its user base.

Zara excels in rapid design, production, and distribution processes, enabling it to bring new fashion trends to market quickly and efficiently, maintaining its competitive edge in fast fashion.

By clearly defining and strategically managing their key activities, companies can ensure that they are not only delivering their value proposition effectively but are also operating in the most efficient and effective manner possible. This alignment is crucial for maintaining competitiveness and achieving sustainable growth in the dynamic business environment.

1.9 Fostering Key Partnerships

The "Key Partnerships" segment of the Business Model Canvas emphasizes the strategic alliances, collaborations, and partnerships that a business forms to optimize its business model, reduce risk, and access resources it might lack internally. These partnerships can be with suppliers, distributors, competitors, government bodies, or other entities. Effective partnerships are often pivotal for businesses to scale operations, enter new markets, and enhance their value propositions.

1.9.1 Strategies for Identifying and Establishing Beneficial Partnerships

Complementarity. Look for partners whose products, services, or resources complement your own. This can lead to synergies that enhance the value proposition for both parties' customer bases.

Market Access. Partner with companies that can provide access to new markets. This could be through established distribution channels, a strong brand presence, or regulatory know-how in a foreign market.

Innovation. Collaborate with entities that can bring in new technologies or innovative business practices. This can help in keeping your offerings competitive and cutting-edge.

Risk and Cost Sharing. Identify partnerships that allow for the sharing of risks and costs, particularly in areas like research and development or market entry strategies. This can make new initiatives more feasible and less burdensome.

Resource Access. Form alliances with businesses or institutions that can offer critical resources, be they physical, intellectual, human, or financial, which are not readily available internally.

Strategic Fit. Ensure that potential partners share similar values and strategic goals. A strong cultural and strategic alignment can significantly improve the chances of partnership success.

1.9.2 Case Studies Highlighting Successful Partnerships

Spotify and Starbucks. In a move to enhance customer experience, Spotify and Starbucks entered into a partnership. Starbucks employees curate playlists that customers can access through Spotify in-store, while Spotify users can earn rewards points for the Starbucks loyalty program. This collaboration leverages Starbucks' presence in daily life and Spotify's digital music platform to mutually enhance brand engagement.

Nike and Apple. A long-standing partnership that began with the Nike+ iPod, combining Nike's expertise in athletic gear with Apple's technological prowess. This partnership has evolved to include integration with the Apple Watch, creating a seamless fitness tracking experience for users and reinforcing the strong brand association between fitness and technology.

Uber and Toyota. Toyota invested in Uber and announced plans to collaborate on the development of autonomous vehicles. This partnership combines Uber's data and platform with Toyota's manufacturing and technology capabilities, aimed at accelerating innovation in the transportation industry.

Google and NASA have partnered on various projects, including the use of Google's quantum computers to optimize space exploration and aeronautics research. This partnership allows Google to test and improve its quantum computing capabilities while providing NASA with access to cutting-edge computational resources.

These case studies illustrate the diverse ways in which strategic partnerships can be leveraged to support business operations, drive growth, and create value. By carefully selecting partners that complement their strengths and compensate for their weaknesses, businesses can forge powerful alliances that propel them towards achieving their strategic goals.

1.10 Analysing Cost Structure

The "Cost Structure" segment of the Business Model Canvas is pivotal for understanding the financial underpinnings of a business's operations. It involves a detailed examination of the fixed and variable costs a business incurs to deliver its value proposition, reach its customer segments, and sustain its key activities and resources. For entrepreneurs and businesses viewing costs as a conundrum, reframing these expenditures as strategic investments is crucial. This perspective not only aids in ensuring financial viability but also in leveraging the cost structure for competitive advantage.

1.10.1 Techniques for Identifying and Managing Major Expenditures

Categorization of Costs. Start by distinguishing between fixed costs (unchanged irrespective of business activity levels, like rent and salaries) and variable costs (fluctuate with business activity, like raw materials and shipping costs). This distinction helps in understanding cost behaviour and managing them more effectively.

Cost-Benefit Analysis. Evaluate each major expenditure in terms of its return on investment (ROI). This involves assessing the direct and indirect benefits of a cost against its financial burden to determine its justification and optimization level.

Adopt lean methodologies to streamline operations and minimize waste across processes. This can include optimizing inventory levels, improving operational efficiencies, and reducing unnecessary overheads.

Outsourcing versus In-house. Analyse activities to determine what can be outsourced cost-effectively versus what should be retained in-house. Outsourcing non-core activities can lead to significant savings and allow the business to focus on its key competencies.

Invest in **technology and automation** to reduce labour costs and improve efficiency. While such investments may have upfront costs, the long-term savings and scalability they offer can be substantial.

Negotiation with Suppliers. Regularly review and negotiate terms with suppliers to ensure you are getting the best prices and terms. Bulk purchasing and long-term contracts can also lead to cost savings.

1.10.2 Insights on Leveraging Cost Structure for Competitive Advantage

Cost Leadership. By achieving a lower cost structure than competitors, a business can offer more competitive pricing to its customers, potentially increasing market share. This requires a continuous focus on cost reduction and efficiency improvements.

Value Innovation. Instead of merely minimizing costs, consider how expenditures can contribute to creating unique value for customers. This could involve investing in superior customer service, product innovation, or quality enhancements that justify a premium pricing strategy (Kim and Mauborgne, 1997).

Flexible Pricing Models. Use your understanding of the cost structure to develop flexible pricing models that can attract different customer segments. This might include tiered pricing, subscriptions, or freemium models that cater to varying willingness to pay.

1.10.3 Real-World Examples

IKEA's cost leadership strategy is achieved through economies of scale, cost-efficient design, a flat-packaging system for logistics efficiency, and self-service warehouses. These strategic cost decisions allow IKEA to offer low prices while maintaining profitability.

Known for its low-cost model, **Southwest Airlines** achieves cost efficiency through standardized flight operations, efficient turnaround times, and a focus on secondary airports. These cost savings enable competitive pricing and profitability in a tough industry.

Tesla's investment in "gigafactories" represents a significant upfront cost but is strategic for long-term cost reduction in battery production, crucial for electric vehicle affordability and the company's competitive edge in the market.

For businesses, especially those navigating the complexities of growth and scalability, viewing costs as investments rather than mere expenses can transform how they approach financial planning and strategic decision-making. This mindset shift enables businesses to align their cost structures with their strategic objectives, thereby turning potential financial burdens into levers for competitive advantage and sustainable success.

1.11 Conclusion: Design for Growth through the Business Model Canvas

As we conclude this chapter within the Design for Growth framework, it's evident that the Business Model Canvas (BMC) is not just a tool but a transformative journey for entrepreneurs and businesses seeking sustainable growth and innovation. The detailed exploration of each BMC segment—from articulating a clear value proposition, understanding customer segments, and cultivating strong relationships, to optimizing channels, defining key activities, unveiling diverse revenue streams, leveraging critical resources, fostering strategic partnerships, and meticulously analysing cost structures—serves as a blueprint for designing a business that is not only viable but also adaptable and resilient.

The BMC as a Dynamic Growth Framework

In the context of Design for Growth, it's crucial to emphasize that the BMC should be approached as a dynamic framework, capable of evolving in tandem with your business. This evolution mirrors the journey of growth and scaling, where adaptability and responsiveness to market conditions and customer needs are paramount. The BMC, therefore, is not a static document but a living strategy that demands regular reflection, reassessment, and refinement.

1.11.1   Continuous Refinement for Sustainable Success

Design for Growth encourages businesses to view the BMC as a continuous loop of learning, innovation, and growth. This iterative process is essential for adapting to the rapidly changing business landscape, driven by technological advances, shifting market demands, and global economic factors. By regularly revisiting each segment of the BMC, businesses can identify new opportunities, anticipate challenges, and pivot their strategies to maintain competitive advantage and relevance.

Embrace a Growth Mindset. Adopting a growth mindset is fundamental to the Design for Growth model. See the BMC as a tool for constant evolution, where every iteration brings your business closer to achieving its full potential.

Innovate with Purpose. Innovation should be purpose-driven, focused on delivering value to customers and solving real problems. Use the BMC to explore how each element of your business model can contribute to a larger vision of impact and success.

Engage in Strategic Experimentation. Encourage experimentation within the safe confines of the BMC framework. Test new ideas, gather data, and learn from both successes and setbacks to refine your business model continuously.

Cultivate Resilience. The journey of growth is fraught with challenges. The BMC provides a structured approach to navigating these challenges, helping businesses to remain resilient, agile, and focused on long-term objectives.

1.11.2   A Call to Action for Growth-Oriented Businesses

This exploration of the BMC within the Design for Growth model is an invitation to entrepreneurs and business leaders to engage deeply with the strategic underpinnings of their operations. It's a call to action to leverage the BMC not just for planning but as a compass for sustained growth, innovation, and competitive differentiation. By integrating the principles of Design for Growth with the structured analysis and flexibility of the BMC, businesses can unlock new levels of success, adaptability, and impact.

In your journey with the BMC, let Design for Growth be your guide, enabling you to navigate the complexities of the business world with clarity, confidence, and a relentless pursuit of excellence. Together, let's design for growth, transforming challenges into opportunities and aspirations into achievements.

1.12 Reflection Questions and Exercises

As we integrate the Business Model Canvas (BMC) into the Design for Growth framework, it becomes crucial to not only understand its components intellectually but to apply these insights practically to your own business. The following reflective questions and exercises are designed to guide you through this application process, encouraging a deeper understanding and actionable insights.

1.12.1 Reflection Questions

Customer Segments:

- Who are your main customer segments, and what specific needs do they have?
- How might these needs evolve, and how can your business adapt to meet them?

Value Proposition:

- What unique value does your business offer to its customers?
- How does your product or service solve problems or fulfill needs differently than competitors?

Channels:

- Through which channels do your customer segments prefer to be reached?
- Are there more efficient or effective channels you could explore to enhance your reach and impact?

Customer Relationships:

- What type of relationship does each of your customer segments expect you to establish and maintain with them?
- How can you enhance these relationships to improve customer loyalty and retention?

Revenue Streams:

- What are your main sources of revenue, and how aligned are they with your value proposition and customer segments?
- Are there untapped revenue streams you could explore to diversify your income?

Key Resources:

- What key resources do you currently leverage, and how do they support your business model?
- Are there additional resources you could utilize to strengthen your business model?

Key Activities:

- What are the most crucial activities required to deliver your value proposition?
- How can these activities be optimized or innovated to enhance efficiency and effectiveness?

Key Partnerships:

- Which partnerships are critical to your business's success?
- How could new partnerships enhance or complement your current business model?

Cost Structure:

- What are the most significant costs in your business model, and how do they drive your value proposition?
- How might you reframe certain costs as investments in growth, and are there areas where costs can be reduced without compromising value?

1.12.2 Exercises

Mapping Your BMC

Create a detailed Business Model Canvas for your current business model. Identify areas of strength and potential areas for improvement.

Scenario Planning

Develop scenarios where market conditions change (e.g., new competitors, changing customer preferences) and use the BMC to strategize potential responses.

Value Proposition Refinement

Draft three different value propositions for your business. Test these with potential or current customers to gain feedback and refine your approach.

Customer Persona Development

Create detailed personas for your key customer segments. Include demographic information, goals, challenges, and how your business addresses their needs.

Partnership Strategy Workshop

Identify potential new partners and conduct a workshop to explore how these partnerships could work. Outline the mutual benefits and how the partnerships could be structured.

Cost Analysis and Optimization

Conduct a thorough review of your cost structure. Identify areas where investments are generating significant returns and areas where costs can be reduced or optimized.

Revenue Stream Innovation

Brainstorm new revenue streams based on your core competencies and key resources. Evaluate these for feasibility and alignment with your overall business model.

By engaging deeply with these reflection questions and exercises, you'll gain a more nuanced understanding of your business model and how it can be adapted and evolved for growth. This hands-on approach encourages you to think creatively and strategically, applying the principles of the Design for Growth framework to forge a path toward sustained success and innovation.

2. Identify Your Business PESTs

2.1 Introduction

In today's intricately connected global economy, businesses face a landscape that is not only dynamic but also shaped by a confluence of forces extending far beyond their immediate market boundaries. The classic PEST analysis, with its focus on Political, Economic, Social, and Technological trends, has been an essential tool for understanding the broad spectrum of external influences on business operations and strategy. It provides a structured framework for analysing the macroeconomic forces and other significant trends that shape the competitive environment, influence consumer behaviour, and impact business performance.

However, the acceleration of environmental concerns and the tightening of regulatory landscapes worldwide have necessitated an expansion of this traditional analysis framework. This evolution has given rise to the PESTEL model, which enriches the original analysis by incorporating Environmental and Legal factors. This broadened perspective is crucial for today's business strategies, as it acknowledges the growing importance of sustainability and the complex web of global and local regulations affecting businesses.

The inclusion of macroeconomic forces within the Economic component of PESTEL is particularly vital. These forces encompass a range of factors, including inflation rates, interest rates, economic growth, unemployment levels, and fiscal policies, all of which exert a profound influence on business operations. Macroeconomic trends can dictate market demand, cost of capital, pricing strategies, and investment decisions, making an in-depth understanding of these forces indispensable for business model innovation.

Moreover, the digital revolution and the ubiquity of the Internet have underscored the significance of PESTEL analysis for businesses of all sizes, including medium-sized enterprises. Digital technologies have transformed market dynamics, customer expectations, and competitive landscapes, necessitating a keen awareness of technological trends and the macroeconomic environment in which these trends unfold.

In this age of global connectivity, external factors such as digital transformation, environmental sustainability, and international regulations have interwoven with macroeconomic forces to create a complex tapestry of challenges and opportunities. Recognizing the relevance of a comprehensive PESTEL analysis, including a deep dive into macroeconomic forces, is critical for businesses aiming to navigate this complexity. It enables them to anticipate changes, formulate resilient strategies, and leverage global trends for competitive advantage.

This chapter explores the evolved PESTEL framework in detail, emphasizing the interplay between macroeconomic forces and other external factors in shaping the future of industries. Through this analysis, businesses can gain insights into the opportunities and threats presented by the global economic landscape, ensuring their business models are well-positioned for success in an ever-changing world.

2.2 The Evolution of PEST to PESTEL Analysis

The journey from PEST to PESTEL analysis marks a significant evolution in the strategic planning landscape, reflecting the increasing complexity and interconnectedness of the global business environment. The PEST analysis, originating in the mid-20th century, emerged as a strategic tool designed to help organizations navigate the vast and varied external factors affecting their operations (Aguilar, 1967). By focusing on Political, Economic, Social, and Technological influences, PEST analysis offered businesses a structured approach to assess the macro-environmental factors that could impact their strategies and operational effectiveness.

2.2.1 Historical Context of PEST Analysis

Initially, PEST analysis was primarily used to scan the external macro-environment for potential threats and opportunities. It allowed businesses to map out the external political, economic, social, and technological landscapes and understand how changes in these areas could influence their competitive position. This analytical framework became an indispensable part of strategic planning processes, enabling organizations to anticipate market shifts and adapt their strategies accordingly.

2.2.2 Rationale for Expanding the Model

As the global business ecosystem evolved, it became increasingly clear that the original PEST framework, while useful, was not comprehensive enough to capture all the critical external factors impacting business operations. Two significant global trends necessitated the expansion of the model: the growing importance of environmental sustainability and the increasingly complex legal and regulatory landscapes.

Environmental Considerations: The late 20th and early 21st centuries saw a rising awareness of environmental issues, such as climate change, resource depletion, and pollution. This growing environmental consciousness among consumers, businesses, and governments highlighted the need for organizations to consider ecological sustainability as a critical external factor. Incorporating Environmental factors into the analysis acknowledges the impact of environmental trends and regulations on business strategies, operations, and competitive advantage.

Legal and Regulatory Dynamics: Simultaneously, businesses were navigating an ever-more-complex web of legal and regulatory requirements, both locally and internationally. This complexity was driven by factors such as globalization, digital transformation, and heightened scrutiny on corporate governance and compliance. The addition of Legal factors to the analysis framework allows businesses to systematically assess the legal and regulatory environment, ensuring compliance and mitigating risks associated with legal challenges and regulatory changes.

2.2.3 PESTEL: A Comprehensive Framework for External Environmental Analysis

The evolution from PEST to PESTEL analysis represents a shift towards a more holistic approach to strategic planning. By including Environmental and Legal factors, the PESTEL framework offers businesses a comprehensive tool for external environmental analysis. This expanded model enables organizations to conduct a more thorough evaluation of the macro-environment, identifying not only threats and opportunities but also highlighting areas for innovation and differentiation.

PESTEL analysis facilitates a deeper understanding of the external forces at play, encouraging businesses to consider a wider range of factors in their strategic planning. This broader perspective is crucial for navigating the complexities of modern markets, ensuring that companies are not only responsive to current trends but also proactive in anticipating future shifts. In essence, the transition from PEST to PESTEL analysis reflects the evolving nature of business strategy, emphasizing the importance of adaptability, sustainability, and compliance in achieving long-term success.

2.3 Political Factors Shaping Business

The political landscape in which a business operates is a critical determinant of its success and sustainability. Political factors, including government policies, regulatory frameworks, trade tariffs, and the overall political climate, can significantly impact business operations, influencing everything from day-to-day functions to strategic decision-making. Understanding and navigating these political realities is essential for businesses aiming to thrive in the global market.

2.3.1 Influence of Political Climates on Business Operations

Government policies and regulations. Governments wield substantial power over business environments through the creation and enforcement of policies and regulations. These can range from tax laws and labor regulations to environmental standards and foreign investment policies. Such regulations can affect operational costs, market accessibility, and competitive dynamics, requiring businesses to be agile and compliant.

Trade tariffs and barriers. Trade policies, including tariffs, quotas, and trade barriers, directly impact a company's ability to operate in international markets. Changes in trade policies can alter the cost structures and supply chains of businesses, affecting pricing, profitability, and strategic partnerships.

Political stability and risk. The degree of political stability within a country can significantly influence business confidence and investment decisions. Political unrest, transitions in power, or policy shifts can introduce uncertainty, affecting market dynamics, investment climates, and business operations.

Governmental support and incentives. On the positive side, governments often offer various programs, incentives, and support to businesses, including grants, tax relief, and infrastructure development. Leveraging these opportunities can provide businesses with a competitive edge and support growth and expansion efforts.

2.3.2 Strategies for Navigating Political Uncertainties

Risk assessment and monitoring. Regularly assess and monitor the political landscape to identify potential risks and opportunities. This can involve tracking policy developments, election outcomes, and geopolitical events that may affect the business environment.

Lobbying and advocacy. Engaging in lobbying efforts or joining industry associations can help influence policy decisions and regulatory frameworks. Effective advocacy can protect business interests and contribute to creating a more favourable operational environment.

Diversifying markets and supply chains can mitigate risks associated with political instability or unfavourable policies in a single country. Exploring new markets can also uncover opportunities for growth beyond politically volatile regions.

Forming **strategic partnerships** with local businesses or entities can provide insights into the political climate and offer additional support in navigating regulatory landscapes. These partnerships can also enhance credibility and facilitate market entry.

Leveraging governmental programs. Stay informed about government incentives and support programs relevant to your industry. These can offer financial advantages, access to resources, and support for innovation and expansion.

By proactively addressing the political factors that influence business operations, companies can better position themselves to manage risks, seize opportunities, and maintain a competitive stance in the face of political uncertainties. Adopting a strategic approach to navigating the political landscape ensures that businesses can adapt and thrive, leveraging governmental programs and policies to their advantage while mitigating the challenges posed by political and regulatory environments.

2.4   Economic Influences on Industry Dynamics

The economic environment plays a pivotal role in shaping industry dynamics and influencing business strategies. Factors such as inflation rates, economic growth, exchange rates, and the overall health of the global economy can significantly impact businesses, affecting everything from consumer purchasing power to operational costs and international competitiveness. Understanding these economic influences is crucial for businesses to navigate the complexities of the market and adapt their strategies for sustained growth and resilience.

2.4.1   Impact of Economic Trends on Business Strategies

Inflation Rates: Inflation can dramatically affect a business's cost structures and pricing strategies. Higher inflation rates may lead to increased costs for raw materials, labour, and other operational expenses. Businesses must adjust their pricing to maintain margins, which can affect consumer demand and overall competitiveness.

The rate of **economic growth** within a country or region influences consumer spending and business investment. In periods of high economic growth, consumer spending typically increases, presenting opportunities for business expansion and increased sales. Conversely, during economic downturns, businesses may need to tighten budgets and focus on efficiency and cost reduction strategies.

For businesses operating in international markets, **exchange rate fluctuations** can have a significant impact on profitability, pricing, and competitive positioning. A stronger domestic currency can make exports more expensive and less competitive abroad, while a weaker currency can boost export competitiveness but increase the cost of imported goods and services.

Global economic interconnectivity. In today's globalised economy, events in one part of the world can have ripple effects across the globe. Economic crises, shifts in trade policies, and geopolitical events can disrupt supply chains, alter commodity prices, and shift market demand. Businesses must be agile and proactive in responding to these global economic shifts to mitigate risks and capitalize on emerging opportunities.

2.4.2 Navigating Economic Influences

Diversifying product offerings and markets can help businesses mitigate risks associated with economic downturns in specific sectors or regions. By having a presence in multiple markets, companies can balance out fluctuations in demand and maintain stable revenue streams.

Developing **flexible pricing strategies** that can adapt to changes in inflation and exchange rates is essential for maintaining competitiveness. This may involve dynamic pricing, cost-plus pricing strategies, or offering value-added services to justify premium prices.

In times of economic uncertainty, focusing on **operational efficiency and cost management** can help businesses maintain profitability. This could involve streamlining processes, adopting new technologies, or renegotiating supplier contracts.

Effective strategic financial planning, including foreign exchange risk management and contingency planning, is crucial for navigating economic volatility. Businesses should regularly review their financial strategies to ensure they are prepared for economic shifts.

Staying informed and agile. Keeping abreast of economic trends and forecasts allows businesses to anticipate changes and adapt their strategies accordingly. Agility in business operations and strategy development is key to responding effectively to economic challenges and opportunities.

By closely monitoring economic trends and understanding their implications, businesses can develop strategies that not only mitigate the risks associated with economic fluctuations but also leverage economic conditions for competitive advantage. The interconnected nature of the global economy requires businesses to be vigilant and adaptable, ready to adjust their operations and strategies in response to changing economic landscapes both locally and internationally.

2.5 Social Trends and Their Impact on Consumer Behaviour

The social fabric of society, characterized by its demographics, cultural norms, and consumer behaviour trends, is in a constant state of flux. These social trends significantly influence consumer preferences, behaviours, and expectations, directly impacting businesses across all sectors. Understanding and adapting to these changes is not just beneficial but essential for companies aiming to stay relevant and competitive in today's dynamic market landscape.

2.5.1 Exploration of Social Trends

Shifts in **demographics**, such as aging populations in some countries and younger demographics in others, influence market demands and consumer preferences. For instance, an aging population may increase the demand for healthcare services, products for older adults, and leisure activities targeted at retirees. Conversely, younger demographics might drive trends in technology adoption, fashion, and entertainment.

Cultural trends, including shifts towards sustainability, health and wellness, and inclusivity, significantly affect consumer behavior. Today's consumers are more environmentally conscious, favoring businesses that prioritize sustainability in their operations and products. Similarly, there is a growing focus on health and wellness, with increased demand for products and services that promote a healthy lifestyle.

Consumer behaviour trends. Advances in technology and the rise of social media have transformed how consumers interact with brands and make purchasing decisions. There is a growing preference for personalized, seamless shopping experiences, both online and offline. Moreover, consumers are increasingly value-driven, supporting brands that demonstrate social responsibility and ethical practices.

2.5.2   Adapting to Social Changes

Businesses must continually **innovate their product and service offerings** to align with evolving consumer needs and preferences. This could involve developing eco-friendly products, integrating advanced technologies for personalized experiences, or offering services that cater to the health and wellness trend.

Effective marketing strategies must reflect the cultural values and social trends relevant to the target audience. This involves using inclusive marketing, highlighting sustainability efforts, and leveraging digital platforms for engagement. Tailoring communication to resonate with the values and interests of different demographic groups can enhance brand relevance and customer loyalty.

Enhancing the customer experience through personalization, convenience, and quality service is crucial in meeting the evolving expectations of consumers. Businesses should leverage data analytics to gain insights into consumer behavior and preferences, enabling them to offer personalized recommendations, streamline the purchasing process, and ensure customer satisfaction.

Engaging in **Corporate Social Responsibility** (CSR) initiatives can significantly impact a business's brand image and appeal to socially conscious consumers. Actions such as adopting sustainable practices, supporting community projects, and ensuring fair trade can differentiate a brand and build consumer trust and loyalty.

Flexibility and responsiveness. Staying attuned to social trends and being responsive to changes in consumer behaviour are key to maintaining competitiveness. Businesses should cultivate a culture of flexibility and innovation, allowing them to quickly adapt their strategies, products, and services to meet the shifting dynamics of the market.

By understanding and strategically responding to social trends and their impact on consumer behaviour, businesses can more effectively meet the needs and preferences of their target audiences. Adapting to social changes not only ensures relevance and competitiveness but also fosters a deeper connection with consumers, ultimately driving growth and success in the ever-evolving market landscape.

2.6 Technological Advancements and Innovation

The relentless pace of technological advancements has become a defining feature of the modern business landscape, with innovations such as digital transformation, artificial intelligence (AI), and the Internet of Things (IoT) reshaping industries at an unprecedented rate. These technological trends offer vast opportunities for businesses to enhance efficiency, create new value propositions, and redefine competitive advantage. However, they also present challenges, as companies must navigate the complexities of integrating new technologies and keep pace with the rapid evolution of the digital world.

2.7 Overview of Technological Trends

Digital transformation involves the integration of digital technology into all areas of a business, fundamentally changing how operations are conducted and value is delivered to customers. It encompasses everything from automating processes and leveraging big data analytics to adopting cloud computing and enhancing online customer experiences.

Artificial Intelligence (AI) and machine learning are at the forefront of technological innovation, offering businesses the tools to automate complex processes, gain insights from data, and enhance decision-making. Applications range from chatbots improving customer service to predictive analytics optimizing supply chain management.

The **Internet of Things (IoT)** connects physical devices to the Internet, enabling data collection and exchange. This connectivity facilitates innovations like smart factories, where machinery and systems can communicate to optimize production, and smart products that offer enhanced functionality and new user experiences.

2.7.1 Leveraging Technology for Competitive Advantage

Technologies like AI and IoT can significantly **enhance operational efficiency** by automating routine tasks, reducing errors, and optimizing resource utilization. This not only lowers operational costs but also allows businesses to focus on innovation and strategic growth.

Creating differentiated value propositions. Digital technologies enable businesses to offer new and unique value propositions. This could be through personalized product recommendations powered by AI, enhanced customer experiences via augmented reality (AR), or new services enabled by IoT connectivity.

Data-driven decision making. The ability to collect, analyse, and act on data is a critical competitive advantage. Technologies like big data analytics and AI provide businesses with insights into customer behaviour, market trends, and operational performance, enabling informed strategic decisions.

2.7.2   Challenges of Keeping Pace with Technological Changes

Resource allocation. Investing in new technologies requires significant resources, both financial and in terms of human capital. Businesses must carefully evaluate which technologies align with their strategic goals and offer the most return on investment.

The rapid evolution of technology can lead to a **skills gap**, where the workforce lacks the necessary expertise to implement and manage new systems. Ongoing training and development, or partnerships with tech providers, can help bridge this gap.

Cybersecurity risks. As businesses become more reliant on digital technologies, the risk of cyber threats increases. Companies must prioritize cybersecurity, protecting their data and systems from breaches that could have devastating financial and reputational consequences.

Regulatory compliance. New technologies often outpace regulatory frameworks, creating uncertainty around issues like data privacy and ethical AI use. Businesses must stay informed about regulatory changes and ensure compliance to avoid legal and ethical pitfalls.

Navigating the world of technological advancements and innovation requires a strategic approach, balancing the potential for competitive advantage with the challenges of rapid change. By staying informed about emerging technologies, investing in digital capabilities, and fostering a culture of agility and innovation, businesses can harness the power of technology to drive growth and success in the digital age.

2.8 Environmental Considerations for Sustainable Business

In the contemporary business landscape, environmental sustainability has transitioned from a niche concern to a central factor in strategic planning and operational decisions. This shift is driven by a combination of increased regulatory pressures, consumer demand for environmentally friendly products, and a growing recognition of the urgent need to address climate change and other environmental challenges. For businesses, integrating sustainability into their operations is not just about compliance or marketing—it's about future-proofing their operations, tapping into new markets, and contributing positively to the planet (Haropoulou and Smallman, 2019).

2.8.1 The Importance of Sustainability and Environmental Regulations

Sustainability as a business imperative. Beyond ethical considerations, sustainability has become a business imperative due to its impact on long-term viability. Companies face risks from resource scarcity, climate change, and environmental degradation, which can disrupt supply chains, increase operational costs, and affect market stability.

Environmental regulations. Globally, governments are enacting stricter environmental regulations to combat pollution, reduce carbon emissions, and encourage sustainable practices. These regulations vary significantly across regions but share a common goal of pushing the business sector toward more sustainable operations.

Consumer demand for green products. Modern consumers are increasingly aware of environmental issues and are showing a strong preference for brands that demonstrate environmental responsibility. This demand influences purchasing decisions, with consumers willing to pay a premium for green products that minimize environmental impacts.

2.8.2 Strategies for Integrating Sustainable Practices

Assessing environmental impact. The first step toward sustainability is understanding your business's environmental impact. This involves assessing all aspects of operations, from raw material sourcing and production processes to packaging and distribution. Life cycle assessments can help identify key areas where improvements can be made.

Adopting eco-friendly materials and processes. Switching to sustainable materials, investing in energy-efficient technologies, and optimizing manufacturing processes can significantly reduce a company's environmental footprint. Renewable energy sources, such as solar or wind power, not only minimize carbon emissions but can also lead to cost savings in the long term.

Waste reduction and recycling. Implementing comprehensive recycling programs and striving for zero waste in operations can enhance sustainability. This might include redesigning products to use fewer materials, repurposing waste products, or participating in circular economy initiatives.

Sustainable supply chain management. Businesses should work closely with suppliers to ensure that their practices align with sustainability goals. This can involve setting environmental standards for suppliers, encouraging the adoption of green practices, and choosing suppliers based on their environmental performance.

Eco-labelling and transparency. Communicating sustainability efforts to consumers through eco-labeling and transparent reporting can build trust and loyalty. Certifications from recognized environmental organizations can also serve as a mark of a company's commitment to sustainability.

Innovating for sustainability. Innovation plays a critical role in achieving sustainability. This can range from developing new eco-friendly products to exploring business models that promote the reuse and recycling of products.

By integrating sustainable practices into their operations, businesses can mitigate their environmental impacts, meet regulatory requirements, and respond to consumer demand for responsible products. Moreover, sustainability can serve as a source of innovation and competitive advantage, opening up new market opportunities and strengthening brand reputation. In an era where environmental considerations are increasingly at the forefront of consumers' minds, the transition to sustainable business practices is not just a moral imperative but a strategic and economic necessity.

2.9 Legal Frameworks and Compliance

In an increasingly globalised business environment, the complexity of legal requirements has become a significant challenge for companies across all industries. From intellectual property rights and data protection laws to labor regulations, navigating the maze of legal obligations is crucial for maintaining operational integrity, safeguarding the business, and ensuring sustainable growth. Understanding these legal frameworks and developing robust compliance strategies are essential steps in mitigating risks and capitalizing on opportunities.

2.9.1 Understanding the Complexity of Legal Requirements

In the digital age, **intellectual property** (IP) has become a critical asset for businesses. Protecting IP rights, including patents, trademarks, copyrights, and trade secrets, is essential for preserving competitive advantage and fostering innovation. However, global operations can complicate IP protection due to varying laws and enforcement mechanisms across jurisdictions.

Data protection laws. With the exponential growth of digital data, data protection has become a paramount concern. Regulations like the General Data Protection Regulation (GDPR) in the European Union set stringent guidelines for data handling and privacy. Businesses must ensure compliance with these laws to avoid substantial fines and reputational damage, necessitating a thorough understanding of data protection requirements in every market they operate.

Labour regulations govern the relationship between employers and employees, including wages, working conditions, and workers' rights. These regulations aim to ensure fair treatment of employees but can vary significantly from one country to another. Compliance with labor laws is not only a legal requirement but also a cornerstone of ethical business practices.

2.9.2 Developing Robust Compliance Strategies

Conducting regular **comprehensive legal audits** can help businesses identify potential compliance issues across all areas of operation. This proactive approach enables companies to address vulnerabilities before they escalate into legal challenges.

Given the rapid pace of legal changes, **staying informed** about relevant laws and regulations is crucial. Businesses should consider subscribing to legal updates, joining industry associations, or consulting with legal experts to keep abreast of developments that could affect their operations.

Educating employees about legal requirements and the importance of compliance is vital. Regular **training** sessions can ensure that staff members are aware of their responsibilities and the legal standards they must uphold in their roles.

Implementing compliance systems. Leveraging technology can streamline compliance management. Systems that automate data protection, monitor IP usage, or track labour law adherence can reduce the burden of manual oversight and enhance compliance efficiency.

Legal partnerships. Building relationships with legal firms or consultants specialising in relevant areas of law can provide valuable insights and guidance. These partnerships can offer timely advice on complex legal issues and help develop strategies to navigate legal challenges effectively.

Integrating legal compliance into the broader **risk management** strategy of the business ensures that legal risks are considered alongside other operational risks. This holistic approach to risk management can protect the business from unforeseen legal challenges and contribute to long-term stability.

Navigating the complexities of legal frameworks and compliance requires a strategic and informed approach. By understanding the legal landscape, staying updated on legal developments, and implementing robust compliance strategies, businesses can protect themselves from legal pitfalls, build trust with stakeholders, and create a foundation for sustainable success in the global market.

2.10 Conducting a PESTEL Analysis for Your Business

A PESTEL analysis is a strategic tool used to systematically understand the macro-environmental factors that may impact your business. It stands for Political, Economic, Social, Technological, Environmental, and Legal factors. This analysis helps businesses to anticipate future trends, adapt their strategies accordingly, and make informed decisions. Here's a step-by-step guide to conducting a PESTEL analysis for your business, along with tips to integrate this process into your strategic planning.

2.10.1 Step-by-Step Guide to Conducting a PESTEL Analysis

Preparation and Scope Definition:

- Begin by defining the scope of your analysis. Determine whether you're conducting the PESTEL analysis for a specific product, service, geographical market, or the business as a whole.
- Identify the objective of the analysis. Understanding what you aim to achieve can help focus the analysis on relevant factors.

Data Collection:

- Collect data relevant to each of the six elements of the PESTEL framework. Use a variety of sources for a comprehensive view, including industry reports, market research, news articles, and government publications.
- Engage stakeholders from different parts of your organization to gather insights and perspectives. This might include interviews or workshops with teams from operations, marketing, finance, and legal departments.

Evaluation:

- Analyse the collected data to identify trends, opportunities, and threats within each PESTEL category.
- Consider how each factor (Political, Economic, Social, Technological, Environmental, Legal) could impact your business, both positively and negatively.

Business Model Development:

- Based on the evaluation, develop potential responses in your business model to the identified opportunities and threats. This could involve diversifying markets, investing in new technologies, adapting marketing strategies, or enhancing compliance mechanisms.
- Prioritize actions based on their potential impact and feasibility. Develop short-term and long-term strategies to address or capitalize on the PESTEL factors.
- We'll cover more of this when we look at evaluating your position and (re)designing for growth.

Integration and Action Plan:

- Integrate the insights from the PESTEL analysis into your business's ongoing business model (value) innovation process. Ensure that the developed strategies are aligned with your overall business goals and objectives.
- Create an action plan detailing the steps needed to implement the business model changes, including timelines, responsibilities, and required resources.

2.10.2 Tips for Integrating PESTEL Analysis into Business Mpdel Innovation

Regular review. Make PESTEL analysis a regular part of your business model innovation process. The macro-environment is constantly changing, and staying updated can help your business remain agile and competitive.

Cross-functional Involvement. Involve team members from across the organization in the PESTEL analysis process. Different perspectives can enrich the analysis and ensure that various aspects of the business are considered.

Identify key indicators for each PESTEL category that are particularly relevant to your business. Regularly **monitor** these indicators to quickly identify changes in the macro-environment.

Use the insights gained from the PESTEL analysis to maintain **business model flexibility**. Be prepared to adapt your strategies in response to significant changes in the macro-environment.

Educate your team about the importance of macro-environmental factors and their potential impact on the business. **Communicate** the findings of the PESTEL analysis and the strategic responses across the organization to ensure alignment and buy-in.

Conducting a PESTEL analysis is a dynamic and ongoing process that can significantly enhance your strategic planning and decision-making. By systematically analysing the external environment and integrating these insights into your business strategy, you can navigate the complexities of the market more effectively and position your business for long-term success.

2.11 Case Studies: Successes and Lessons Learned

Understanding the practical implications of PESTEL analysis can be greatly enhanced by examining real-world case studies. These examples not only showcase the strategic value of adapting to macro-environmental factors but also highlight the risks of failing to do so. Here, we explore both successes and lessons learned from businesses that have navigated the complexities of the PESTEL framework.

2.11.1 Successes in Navigating PESTEL Factors

Tesla, Inc. - Embracing Environmental and Technological Changes:

Tesla has successfully leveraged Environmental and Technological factors to position itself as a leader in the electric vehicle (EV) market. Recognizing the growing consumer demand for sustainable transportation and the global shift towards stricter environmental regulations, Tesla invested heavily in EV technology and sustainable energy solutions. This strategic focus not only aligned with environmental trends but also capitalized on technological advancements in battery and renewable energy, driving growth and innovation.

Airbnb - Adapting to Legal and Social Shifts:

Airbnb's business model faced significant challenges from Legal factors, including regulatory hurdles in various cities and concerns over housing markets. By engaging with policymakers and communities, Airbnb adapted its platform to address these issues, introducing features like the "One Host, One Home" policy in New York City. Additionally, Airbnb tapped into Social trends towards unique and local travel experiences, differentiating itself in the competitive lodging market.

2.11.2 Lessons Learned from Failure to Adapt

Blockbuster - Ignoring Technological and Social Changes:

Blockbuster's failure to adapt to Technological and Social changes offers a cautionary tale. The rise of digital streaming services and changing consumer preferences towards online entertainment were clear trends that Blockbuster failed to adequately respond to. This lack of adaptation led to the company's decline, overshadowed by competitors like Netflix that embraced technological innovations and understood the social shift towards on-demand entertainment.

Kodak - Overlooking Digital Innovation:

Kodak, once a giant in the photography industry, serves as an example of a business that failed to adapt to Technological changes. Despite developing the first digital camera, Kodak was slow to pivot its business model away from film photography to digital, underestimating the speed and impact of digital technology on the photography market. This oversight resulted in Kodak losing its market dominance and filing for bankruptcy in 2012.

2.11.3 Strategic Insights and Takeaways

Successful businesses **anticipate and adapt** to changes in the PESTEL factors proactively. Agility in strategic planning and execution is crucial for capitalizing on opportunities and mitigating risks.

Regularly monitoring the external environment for shifts in PESTEL factors can provide early warning signs of potential challenges and opportunities, allowing businesses to adjust their strategies accordingly.

Engaging with stakeholders, including customers, policymakers, and communities, can provide valuable insights into the implications of PESTEL factors and inform more effective and responsive strategies.

Innovation should be a key response to changes in the macro-environment. Whether it's technological innovation, new business models, or innovative products and services, staying ahead requires continuous innovation.

Learning from failures (moments of truth). Businesses that fail to adapt offer valuable lessons on the importance of responsiveness to the PESTEL factors. Understanding these failures can reinforce the need for vigilance and flexibility in strategic planning.

By examining these case studies, businesses can gain insights into the strategic importance of effectively navigating PESTEL factors. Success in today's dynamic environment requires not just understanding these external influences but actively incorporating this understanding into strategic planning and operational decisions.

2.12 Conclusion

Throughout this exploration of the PESTEL framework, we've delved into the multifaceted external environment that shapes the terrain for businesses across the globe. From political shifts and economic fluctuations to social trends, technological breakthroughs, environmental concerns, and legal frameworks, it's clear that a myriad of factors plays a critical role in defining opportunities and challenges in the business landscape. The PESTEL analysis emerges not just as a tool but as a strategic imperative, enabling businesses to dissect and understand these complex external influences.

The call to action for businesses, particularly medium-sized enterprises, cannot be overstated. In an era marked by rapid changes and unforeseen challenges, the regular incorporation of PESTEL analyses into business model innovation is essential. This practice allows businesses to proactively identify opportunities for growth and innovation while simultaneously mitigating risks. By understanding the external factors at play, businesses can develop strategies that are both resilient and adaptive, ensuring they remain competitive and relevant.

Moreover, it is crucial for businesses to recognize that PESTEL analysis is not a static exercise but a dynamic component of business modelling. As the global business environment continues to evolve, so too should the strategies businesses employ to navigate it. The PESTEL framework offers a lens through which to continuously reassess the landscape, ensuring that businesses can pivot and adapt in response to emerging trends and changes.

2.13 Reflection Questions and Exercises

Identify Changes

What are the most significant changes occurring in each PESTEL category (Political, Economic, Social, Technological, Environmental, Legal) that could impact your industry? How might these changes affect your business model?

Assess Impact

For each identified change, assess its potential impact on your business. Which aspects of your operations are most at risk, and where do you see opportunities for growth or innovation?

Strategic Alignment

How well-aligned is your current business strategy with the findings from your PESTEL analysis? Identify areas in your business model where adjustments may be necessary to better respond to external changes.

Action Plan

Develop an action plan to address the most critical issues identified in your PESTEL analysis. Who will be responsible for each action, and what timelines will you set for implementation?

Monitoring Mechanism

What mechanisms will you put in place to regularly monitor external changes in each of the PESTEL categories? How will you ensure that your business remains responsive to these changes over time?

By engaging with these reflective questions and exercises, businesses can deepen their understanding of the external factors affecting their industry and refine their strategic approaches accordingly. The PESTEL analysis, when utilized as an ongoing tool for strategic planning, empowers businesses to navigate the complexities of the external environment with confidence and agility, paving the way for sustained success and growth.

3. Build Competitive Intelligence

3.1 Introduction

In the rapidly evolving and fiercely competitive business landscape of today, the ability to gather, analyse, and act upon competitive intelligence (CI) has become a cornerstone of strategic planning and operational success. The intricate process of building CI draws inspiration from an unconventional source: the rigorous and strategic discipline of paramilitary situation analysis. This approach, grounded in the principles of vigilance, strategic foresight, and adaptability, offers a fresh lens through which businesses can view and navigate the complex dynamics of industry and market forces.

CI, in its essence, is the systematic gathering, analysis, and application of information about competitors, market trends, technological advancements, and the broader external environment. By adopting a methodology akin to situation analysis used in paramilitary contexts, businesses can achieve a more profound and nuanced understanding of the forces shaping their competitive landscape. This perspective emphasises not just the collection of data, but a keen interpretation of how various elements—ranging from global economic trends to subtle shifts in consumer behaviour—interconnect and impact business strategy.

The value of this approach lies in its ability to transform disparate pieces of information into a coherent picture of the external environment. It enables businesses to anticipate changes, identify emerging threats and opportunities, and craft strategies that are both proactive and responsive. By fostering a culture of personal and team situation awareness, companies can cultivate a dynamic competitive intelligence capability. This capability is crucial for staying ahead in the game, ensuring that businesses are not merely reacting to their competitors' moves, but are actively shaping the competitive dialogue.

In this chapter, we will explore how competitive intelligence, informed by the principles of situation analysis, equips businesses to deeply understand and effectively respond to industry forces (such as suppliers, stakeholders, incumbent competitors, new entrants, and substitute products and services) and market forces (including market segments, customer needs and demand, challenges, switching costs, and revenue attractiveness). Through this approach, businesses can develop a strategic edge that is both comprehensive and finely tuned to the nuances of their operational theater, ensuring they are well-positioned to navigate the complexities of the modern market landscape.

3.2 The Foundations of Situation Analysis in Competitive Intelligence

Situation analysis, a concept deeply rooted in paramilitary strategy, has found a significant place in the realm of business competitive intelligence (CI). Originally designed to assess the operational environment, anticipate potential threats, and identify strategic opportunities in military contexts, situation analysis offers a rigorous framework for understanding the complexities of the competitive business landscape. This section explores the adaptation of this strategic tool for CI, emphasizing the importance of a holistic view of both internal and external business environments.

3.2.1 From Paramilitary Strategy to Business Application

In paramilitary organizations, situation analysis is a critical process used to evaluate the current state of the operational environment, encompassing a broad spectrum of factors such as enemy positioning, terrain analysis, and resource availability. The core objective is to ensure preparedness and strategic advantage in a constantly changing and often adversarial environment. Translating this concept into a business context involves analysing the competitive landscape with a similar level of rigor and strategic foresight. Businesses adopt this approach to systematically examine market dynamics, competitor behaviours, customer trends, and other external forces that impact their operations and strategic decisions.

The application of situation analysis in business CI involves a continuous cycle of gathering relevant data, analysing this information to uncover actionable insights, and applying these insights to inform strategic planning and decision-making. This process enables businesses to stay ahead of industry trends, anticipate competitor moves, and adapt to market changes with agility.

3.2.2 Comprehensive Understanding of Business Environments

The essence of leveraging situation analysis for CI lies in its comprehensive approach to understanding both internal and external environments that affect a business:

- **External Environment Analysis** includes examining market trends, industry forces, regulatory landscapes, technological advancements, and competitive dynamics. By understanding these external factors, businesses can identify threats and opportunities in the broader market, enabling them to position themselves strategically against competitors and align their offerings with market demands.
- **Internal Environment Analysis**. Equally important is an introspective look at the organization's internal capabilities, resources, processes, and culture. This analysis helps identify strengths to be leveraged and weaknesses to be addressed, ensuring that the business is internally equipped to execute its competitive strategies effectively.

A comprehensive situation analysis recognizes that external market opportunities are only advantageous if the organization possesses the internal capabilities to capitalize on them. Similarly, understanding competitive threats requires an assessment of internal vulnerabilities that may need to be mitigated.

The integration of situation analysis into CI practices empowers businesses to develop a nuanced and multi-dimensional understanding of their operational landscape. It encourages a proactive stance towards competition, where strategic moves are informed by a deep and holistic analysis of both the battlefield and the organization's own arsenal. By adopting principles from paramilitary strategy, businesses can navigate the complexities of the competitive environment more effectively, making informed decisions that drive sustainable growth and competitive advantage.

3.3 Developing Personal Situation Awareness

In the realm of competitive intelligence, personal situation awareness acts as the initial beacon, guiding the strategic direction through the murky waters of market dynamics, competitor maneuvers, and evolving customer needs. Enhancing this individual acuity is pivotal for professionals at all levels, enabling them to contribute valuable insights to their organization's collective intelligence framework. Here, we delve into techniques, practices, and tools essential for sharpening personal situation awareness.

3.3.1 Techniques for Enhancing Awareness

Active Monitoring of Market Trends

Regularly engage with industry reports, trade journals, and market research studies to keep abreast of broader market trends and shifts. This habit helps in understanding the macroeconomic forces and industry-specific developments influencing market dynamics.

Competitor Analysis

Develop a routine for tracking competitor activities, including product launches, marketing campaigns, strategic moves, and financial performance. Social media platforms, company websites, and financial news outlets are rich sources of such information.

Customer Feedback Loops

Actively seek out customer feedback through surveys, social media listening, and direct engagement. Understanding customer preferences and pain points is crucial for anticipating shifts in market demand and identifying unmet needs.

3.3.2 The Role of Continuous Learning

The landscape of business is in perpetual motion, driven by technological advancements, regulatory changes, and evolving consumer behaviours. Engaging in continuous learning through online courses, webinars, industry conferences, and professional networking helps individuals stay informed and adaptable to these changes.

3.3.3 Market Research and Environmental Scanning

Market research and environmental scanning are systematic approaches to gather actionable data on the external environment. These practices involve:

Quantitative Research: Surveys and statistical analyses to gauge market trends, customer behaviours, and industry benchmarks.

Qualitative Research: Interviews, focus groups, and case studies to gain deeper insights into customer motivations and competitor strategies.

Environmental Scanning: A regular review of the political, economic, social, technological, environmental, and legal (PESTEL) factors that could impact the business.

3.3.4   Tools and Technologies for Competitive Intelligence

Digital Analytics Platforms

Tools like Google Analytics, SEMrush, and SimilarWeb offer insights into online consumer behaviors, website traffic, and digital marketing effectiveness.

Social Media Monitoring Tools

Platforms such as Hootsuite, BuzzSumo, and Mention enable professionals to track mentions of their brand, competitors, and industry trends across social media channels.

Competitive Intelligence Software

Specialized CI software solutions, such as Crayon and Kompyte, provide comprehensive analysis capabilities for tracking competitor activities and market changes.

Customer Relationship Management (CRM) Systems

CRM systems can be invaluable for compiling customer interactions, preferences, and feedback, offering a centralized repository of customer insights.

By integrating these techniques, practices, and tools into their professional routines, individuals can significantly enhance their personal situation awareness. This heightened awareness is instrumental in identifying early signs of opportunity or threat, enabling businesses to formulate proactive strategies. Cultivating personal awareness not only contributes to the individual's professional development but also enriches the organization's competitive intelligence, ensuring a more agile and informed approach to strategic decision-making.

3.4   Transforming Personal Awareness into Team Intelligence

The transition from individual acuity to a reservoir of team intelligence marks a pivotal evolution in the strategic capability of an organization. This collective intelligence, born from the amalgamation of diverse personal insights, empowers teams to navigate complex competitive landscapes with agility and foresight. Below, we delve into strategies for fostering this transformation, the importance of communication and collaboration, and real-world examples of this dynamic in action.

3.4.1   Strategies for Sharing Personal Insights

Regular Intelligence Sharing Meetings

Implement routine sessions dedicated to sharing market insights, competitor updates, and customer feedback gathered by team members. These meetings encourage the exchange of information and ensure that valuable intelligence is disseminated across the team.

Collaborative Digital Platforms

Utilize digital collaboration tools such as Slack, Microsoft Teams, or Trello to create dedicated channels for competitive intelligence sharing. These platforms facilitate real-time information exchange and can be invaluable in maintaining an up-to-date repository of insights.

Cross-Functional Workshops

Organize workshops that bring together team members from different functional areas to discuss insights and perspectives. These sessions can help in identifying patterns, opportunities, and threats that might not be evident from a single viewpoint.

3.4.2   The Role of Effective Communication and Collaboration

Building a Culture of Openness

Cultivating an environment where team members feel valued and encouraged to share their observations is crucial. This openness enhances trust and ensures a more comprehensive understanding of the competitive landscape.

Diversity of Perspectives

Encourage team members to share insights based on their unique backgrounds, expertise, and viewpoints. This diversity enriches the collective intelligence and leads to more innovative and robust strategic decisions.

Synthesizing Insights

Effective collaboration involves not just sharing information but actively synthesizing diverse insights to uncover actionable intelligence. Techniques such as brainstorming, SWOT analysis, and scenario planning can help in this synthesis.

3.4.3   Case Studies

IBM's Shift to Cloud Computing

Background

IBM, once primarily known for its hardware, faced significant market shifts with the rise of cloud computing and AI. Observing these trends, individual team members across the organization noted the increasing demand for cloud services and data analytics.

Transformation

These insights were collectively analysed, leading IBM to pivot its strategy towards cloud computing and artificial intelligence. By fostering a culture of open communication, IBM effectively transformed these personal observations into a strategic roadmap that emphasized cloud services like IBM Cloud and Watson AI.

Outcome

This strategic pivot allowed IBM to remain competitive in a rapidly evolving tech landscape, leveraging its legacy in hardware and software to become a leader in the cloud computing space.

Lego's Digital and Market Innovation

Background

In the early 2000s, Lego faced a significant downturn, with changing consumer behaviours and digital entertainment threatening traditional toy sales. Insights from market research, customer feedback, and digital trends highlighted by individual employees pointed towards the need for innovation.

Transformation

Lego harnessed these insights to embrace digital transformation and co-creation with customers. Initiatives such as Lego Ideas, where customers could submit and vote on new product ideas, and the expansion into digital games and movies, were direct results of synthesizing team intelligence.

Outcome

These moves revitalized the brand, tapping into new revenue streams while staying true to its core product. Lego's ability to adapt based on collective intelligence transformed it into one of the most powerful toy brands globally.

Starbucks' Response to Consumer Preferences

Background

Starbucks, monitoring evolving consumer preferences towards health and sustainability, recognized the need to adapt its offerings. Team members from various regions observed a growing demand for dairy-free alternatives and environmentally friendly practices.

Transformation

By integrating these insights across the organization, Starbucks expanded its menu to include plant-based milk options and launched initiatives to reduce waste, such as the elimination of plastic straws. These changes were informed by a company-wide commitment to leveraging collective insights for strategic decision-making.

Outcome

The introduction of these options not only catered to the changing consumer preferences but also positioned Starbucks as a forward-thinking, environmentally conscious brand. This responsiveness to customer needs helped maintain its market leadership in the competitive coffee industry.

These examples underscore the value of transforming personal awareness into collective team intelligence. By fostering environments where insights are shared and acted upon, businesses like IBM, Lego, and Starbucks have successfully navigated market shifts and consumer trends, securing their competitive edge and driving innovation.

These case studies exemplify how individual observations, when effectively shared and synthesized within a team, can transform into collective intelligence that drives strategic innovation and competitive advantage. The key lies in fostering an environment of open communication and collaboration, where diverse insights are valued and leveraged to navigate the complexities of the competitive landscape. By prioritizing the transformation of personal awareness into team intelligence, organizations can ensure they are not just reacting to market changes but proactively shaping their strategic destiny.

3.5 Effective Communication and Collaboration

In today's fast-paced and complex business environment, the ability to communicate effectively and collaborate seamlessly is more critical than ever. These capabilities enable teams to harness collective intelligence, make informed decisions rapidly, and maintain a competitive edge. Below, we explore best practices, techniques, and tools that facilitate effective communication and collaboration within organizations.

3.5.1 Best Practices for Fostering an Open Environment

Encourage an atmosphere where team members feel valued and respected. **Trust** is the cornerstone of open communication; when team members trust each other, they are more likely to share ideas, concerns, and insights freely.

Leaders should model **transparency** by openly sharing information about decisions, strategies, and challenges. This practice sets a precedent for open communication throughout the organization.

Define and communicate the preferred channels for different types of **communication** (e.g., email for formal communications, instant messaging for quick questions). Clear guidelines help prevent misunderstandings and ensure that important information is shared effectively.

3.5.2   Techniques for Overcoming Barriers

Encourage team members to practice **active listening**, which involves fully concentrating, understanding, responding, and then remembering what is being said. This technique helps in acknowledging different viewpoints and fosters a more inclusive environment.

Implement regular **feedback loops** where team members can express their thoughts on communication and collaboration practices. Use this feedback to make continuous improvements.

Develop and communicate clear **mechanisms for conflict resolution** to address and resolve misunderstandings or disagreements constructively, without stifling open communication.

3.5.3   Tools and Platforms for Enhancing Communication and Collaboration

Collaborative Work Management Platforms

These tools (e.g., Asana, Trello) help teams organize projects, assign tasks, track progress, and communicate updates in a centralized location, enhancing transparency and accountability.

Instant Messaging and Team Collaboration Software

Instant messaging platforms (e.g., Slack, Microsoft Teams) facilitate real-time communication, quick information exchange, and informal discussions, fostering a sense of community and immediacy in team interactions.

Video Conferencing Tools

Video conferencing platforms (e.g., Zoom, Google Meet) have become essential for maintaining face-to-face communication, especially in remote or distributed teams. They are crucial for team meetings, brainstorming sessions, and building relationships.

Document and File Sharing Services

Cloud-based document and file-sharing services (e.g., Google Drive, Dropbox) enable teams to collaborate on documents in real time, ensuring that everyone has access to the latest information and can contribute simultaneously.

Idea Management Software

These platforms (e.g., IdeaScale, Brightidea) allow organizations to crowdsource ideas from employees, providing a structured way to submit, discuss, and develop ideas. They can be instrumental in leveraging collective intelligence for innovation.

By implementing these best practices, techniques, and tools, organizations can create an environment that not only fosters open communication and effective collaboration but also empowers teams to synthesize diverse perspectives into actionable insights. This collaborative culture is essential for developing competitive intelligence, making strategic decisions, and navigating the complexities of the modern business landscape with agility and innovation.

3.6 Leveraging Collective Intelligence for Strategic Advantage

Collective intelligence, the combined knowledge and insights of a team or organization, is a powerful asset in the competitive business landscape. When harnessed effectively, it enables teams to anticipate competitive moves, identify strategic opportunities, and maintain a competitive edge through informed decision-making. This section explores how teams can leverage their collective intelligence for strategic advantage, emphasizing adaptability, quick response, and the importance of ongoing intelligence gathering.

3.6.1 Anticipating Competitive Moves

Engage in scenario planning exercises that utilize the diverse perspectives within the team to envision possible future states. This practice helps in anticipating potential competitive moves and preparing strategic responses.

Conduct war gaming sessions, where team members role-play competitors and market actors. This interactive approach provides insights into competitors' possible strategies and how they might react to your business moves.

Establish a routine for continuous monitoring and analysis of competitor activities. By pooling insights from various team members, organizations can quickly identify patterns or shifts in competitor strategies.

3.6.2 Identifying Strategic Opportunities

Foster collaboration across different functional areas of the organization to combine insights from marketing, sales, R&D, and operations. This cross-pollination of ideas can uncover unique opportunities at the intersection of disciplines.

Utilize open innovation platforms where employees, and sometimes even customers and partners, can submit ideas for new products, services, or improvements. This democratized approach to idea generation can surface opportunities that might not emerge through traditional channels.

Regularly analyse market trends and consumer behaviour changes as a team. Leveraging the collective intelligence to interpret these trends can reveal emerging opportunities and guide the strategic direction.

3.6.3 Adaptability and Quick Response

Develop agile decision-making processes that allow the organization to act quickly on the insights derived from collective intelligence. This may involve empowering lower-level teams to make decisions or creating rapid-response teams for emerging opportunities.

Implement feedback loops that continuously evaluate the outcomes of decisions and strategies. These loops provide real-time learning that can inform future actions and adjustments.

3.6.4 Maintaining a Competitive Edge

Commit to **ongoing situation analysis** that routinely scans the external environment for changes in the PESTEL factors (Political, Economic, Social, Technological, Environmental, and Legal). This ongoing vigilance helps in adapting strategies to evolving market conditions.

Invest in **knowledge management systems** that capture, store, and disseminate insights throughout the organization. These systems ensure that valuable intelligence is accessible and can be acted upon by all relevant stakeholders.

Cultivate a **culture of continuous learning** where team members are encouraged to update their knowledge, share insights, and stay curious about industry developments and emerging technologies.

By leveraging collective intelligence, teams can not only react to the competitive landscape but proactively shape it. The key lies in fostering an environment that encourages the sharing of insights, promotes adaptability, and emphasizes the strategic value of ongoing intelligence gathering. In doing so, organizations can secure a strategic advantage that is both dynamic and sustainable, ensuring they remain ahead in the game.

3.7 Applying Competitive Intelligence to Industry Analysis

Competitive intelligence (CI) plays a crucial role in understanding and navigating the complex dynamics of industry landscapes. By systematically gathering, analysing, and applying information about suppliers, stakeholders, incumbent competitors, new entrants, and substitute products and services, businesses can gain strategic insights that inform decision-making and strategy development. This section outlines how CI can be effectively applied to industry analysis, providing strategies for leveraging CI to understand industry trends and forecast potential shifts.

3.7.1 Analysing Industry Dynamics

Suppliers and Supply Chain Analysis

Use CI to assess the stability, reliability, and bargaining power of suppliers. Understanding the supply chain landscape helps in identifying potential vulnerabilities or opportunities for cost optimization and innovation.

Stakeholder Mapping and Analysis

Identify and analyse key stakeholders within the industry, including regulatory bodies, advocacy groups, and strategic partners. CI can uncover stakeholders' interests, influence, and potential impact on business operations, guiding engagement strategies.

Competitor Benchmarking

Comprehensive competitor analysis is a cornerstone of CI. This involves monitoring incumbent competitors' strategies, performance, strengths, and weaknesses. CI tools can help benchmark your business against competitors to identify areas for improvement and differentiation.

Monitoring New Entrants

Keep a close eye on potential and actual new entrants to the industry. CI provides insights into their capabilities, strategies, and potential impact on market dynamics. This awareness is vital for developing pre-emptive strategies to maintain competitive advantage.

Assessing Substitute Products and Services

Analyse the landscape for substitute products and services that could meet similar customer needs. Understanding the threat of substitutes helps in refining value propositions and identifying areas for innovation.

3.7.2   Leveraging CI for Industry Trend Analysis and Forecasting

Trend Spotting

Utilize CI to spot emerging trends in the industry, whether they are technological advancements, shifts in consumer preferences, or regulatory changes. Early identification of trends allows businesses to adapt and innovate proactively.

Scenario Planning

Apply insights from CI to engage in scenario planning, envisioning possible future states of the industry based on current trends and potential disruptions. This exercise aids in preparing for various market conditions, minimizing risks, and seizing opportunities.

Predictive Analysis

Employ advanced analytics and data modeling techniques to forecast potential industry shifts. CI data, when analyzed with predictive tools, can provide a forward-looking perspective, guiding strategic planning and investment decisions.

Continuous Monitoring and Feedback Loops

Establish mechanisms for the ongoing monitoring of industry dynamics and the effectiveness of strategic responses. This ensures that the CI process is adaptive and responsive to changes in the industry landscape.

3.7.3   Strategic Application of CI Insights

Incorporating CI into business growth activities involves translating insights into actionable strategies. This could mean diversifying the supply chain to reduce risks identified through supplier analysis, innovating product offerings in response to the threat of substitutes, or adjusting market positioning based on competitor benchmarking outcomes.

Effective application of CI to industry analysis not only enhances a business's ability to respond to current market conditions but also positions it to anticipate and shape future industry trends. By maintaining a comprehensive and forward-looking view of the industry landscape, businesses can develop resilient strategies that ensure long-term competitive advantage and sustained growth.

3.8 Leveraging Competitive Intelligence for Market Analysis

Deploying CI effectively for market analysis allows businesses to deeply understand their target segments, customer needs, market challenges, and the overall revenue potential of different markets. This strategic application of CI equips organizations with the insights needed to tailor their offerings, anticipate market shifts, and sustain a competitive advantage. Below are strategies and techniques for leveraging CI in market analysis, focusing on monitoring trends and adapting to market changes.

3.8.1 Gaining Insights into Market Segments and Customer Needs

Segmentation Analysis

Use CI to segment the market based on various criteria, including demographic, psychographic, and behavioral factors. This helps in identifying the most lucrative segments and understanding their specific needs and preferences.

Customer Needs Assessment

Deploy surveys, focus groups, and social media analysis to gather direct insights into customer needs, pain points, and expectations. CI tools can also track online behaviour and purchase patterns to offer a granular view of customer preferences.

Demand Forecasting

Apply CI to predict future demand trends in your target segments. Analysing past sales data, market trends, and economic indicators can help forecast demand, guiding inventory management and marketing strategies.

3.8.2 Understanding Market Challenges and Revenue Attractiveness

Competitive Landscape Mapping

Identify and analyze the key players in each market segment, their market share, strengths, and weaknesses. Understanding the competitive landscape helps in identifying market gaps and opportunities for differentiation.

Barriers to Entry and Market Challenges

CI provides insights into potential barriers to entry, such as regulatory hurdles, high capital requirements, or entrenched competitors. Identifying these challenges early on allows for strategic planning to overcome or circumvent them.

Revenue Potential Analysis

Assess the revenue attractiveness of different market segments by analyzing size, growth potential, profitability, and competitive intensity. CI tools can help estimate the potential return on investment for entering or expanding within a segment.

3.8.3 Monitoring Market Trends and Adapting to Changes

Real-time Trend Monitoring

Leverage digital tools and platforms for real-time monitoring of market trends, consumer sentiments, and emerging technologies. Staying abreast of these trends ensures that businesses can quickly adapt to market shifts.

Scenario Planning

Utilize insights from CI to develop scenarios based on potential market developments. Scenario planning aids in preparing for various futures, allowing businesses to respond swiftly and effectively to changes.

Adaptive Strategy Development

Incorporate flexibility into strategic planning, allowing for quick pivots in response to new CI insights. This might involve diversifying product lines, adjusting pricing strategies, or shifting marketing focus.

3.8.4 Techniques for Effective CI in Market Analysis

Social Listening Platforms. Tools like Brandwatch and Mention provide real-time insights into consumer discussions, sentiment, and trends across social media and the web.

Market Research Databases. Access to comprehensive databases like Statista or IBISWorld offers detailed industry reports, market statistics, and forecasts that inform market analysis.

Analytics and BI Tools. Utilizing business intelligence (BI) tools like Tableau or Google Analytics enables the visualization and analysis of market data, enhancing decision-making processes.

By systematically applying competitive intelligence to market analysis, businesses can gain a nuanced understanding of their operational landscape, enabling them to anticipate market needs, navigate challenges, and capitalize on revenue opportunities. This strategic approach ensures that organizations not only react to market dynamics but proactively shape their strategies to meet evolving customer demands and maintain a competitive edge.

3.9 Building a Competitive Intelligence Framework

Creating a structured competitive intelligence (CI) framework is essential for businesses aiming to systematically gather, analyze, and leverage insights for strategic advantage. This framework enables organizations to stay ahead of industry trends, anticipate competitor moves, and make informed decisions. Below are the steps to establish a CI framework, the importance of leadership in these efforts, and strategies for measuring its impact.

3.9.1 Steps for Establishing a CI Framework

Define Objectives and Scope

Clearly articulate the goals of your CI efforts. What strategic questions do you need to answer? Which competitors, market segments, or technological trends are most relevant to your strategic planning?

Gather Intelligence

Determine the sources of information you will tap into, which may include industry reports, social media, patent filings, and direct competitor observation. Establish routines for regular intelligence gathering.

Analyse and Synthesise Information

Develop methodologies for analysing the gathered intelligence. This may involve SWOT analysis, trend spotting, or scenario planning. The key is to transform raw data into actionable insights.

Disseminate Insights

Ensure that the insights reach the relevant decision-makers in a timely and accessible manner. This might involve regular intelligence briefings, dashboards, or integrated reports.

Integrate into Strategic Planning

Use the insights derived from the CI process to inform strategic planning sessions, risk management, and opportunity assessment. Ensure that CI informs both long-term strategy and immediate tactical decisions.

Review and Adapt

Regularly review the effectiveness of your CI process. What insights have been most valuable? How can the process be improved to better meet strategic needs?

3.9.2 Leadership's Role in Championing CI

Leadership must actively advocate for and support CI efforts, recognizing its value in strategic planning and decision-making. This includes providing the necessary resources and integrating CI insights into executive discussions.

Encourage a culture of curiosity and informed decision-making. Leaders should model the use of CI in their strategies, demonstrating its importance and encouraging its use throughout the organization.

Ensure that CI efforts are aligned with the organization's strategic goals. Leadership should regularly consult with the CI team to understand emerging threats and opportunities.

3.9.3 Measuring the Impact of CI

Assess how CI has influenced key strategic decisions. Were certain pitfalls avoided or opportunities seized because of insights gained through CI?

Develop metrics to evaluate the performance of the CI process, such as the timeliness of intelligence reports, the accuracy of forecasts, or the ROI of decisions informed by CI.

Implement feedback mechanisms to gather input from CI users on its effectiveness and areas for improvement. This can help refine the process and ensure it remains aligned with business needs.

Compare your CI outcomes against industry benchmarks or competitors where possible. This can provide an external perspective on the effectiveness of your CI efforts.

Building a comprehensive CI framework is not a one-time effort but an ongoing process that evolves with the business and its strategic needs. Leadership plays a crucial role in embedding CI into the organizational fabric, ensuring it drives informed decision-making and strategic advantage. By systematically gathering, analysing, applying, and measuring the impact of competitive intelligence, businesses can navigate the complexities of the market with greater confidence and agility.

3.10 Conclusion

The journey through the intricacies of building competitive intelligence (CI) through situation analysis has underscored its indispensable role in today's business landscape. This exploration has illuminated the multifaceted approach required to navigate the complexities of modern markets, emphasizing the transition from personal awareness to a cohesive team intelligence strategy. The critical importance of CI in strategic planning cannot be overstated—it is the beacon that guides businesses through turbulent waters, enabling them to anticipate changes, recognize opportunities, and effectively counter competitive threats.

As we conclude, it is imperative to issue a call to action for businesses across all sectors to prioritize the cultivation of personal and team situation awareness within their competitive strategies. This awareness is the foundation upon which robust competitive intelligence is built. It begins with the individual—each team member's capacity to observe, analyse, and interpret the myriad signals in the external environment. However, its true power is realized when these individual insights are amalgamated, forming a comprehensive intelligence that can inform strategic decision-making and drive competitive advantage.

Moreover, businesses are encouraged to foster a culture that values observation, open communication, and collaboration. Such a culture not only facilitates the seamless flow of information but also ensures that diverse perspectives are heard and integrated into the collective understanding. This environment is crucial for nurturing the agility and responsiveness that today's competitive landscape demands.

The benefits of a well-structured CI process, grounded in situation analysis and enriched by collective team insights, are manifold. Organizations that succeed in this endeavour are better positioned to anticipate market shifts, innovate proactively, and respond dynamically to competitors' moves. They can navigate challenges with greater confidence and seize opportunities that others may overlook.

In essence, the ability to harness and leverage competitive intelligence is not merely a tactical asset but a strategic imperative. It distinguishes leaders from followers in the competitive arena, empowering businesses to chart a course toward sustained success and growth. Let this exploration serve as a blueprint for integrating CI into your strategic framework, inspiring your organization to cultivate the awareness, acuity, and agility that define competitive excellence.

As we move forward, let us embrace the ethos of continuous learning, vigilant observation, and strategic foresight. In doing so, we ensure that our businesses are not merely participants in the market but formidable architects of their own destiny, adeptly steering through the ever-evolving landscape with intelligence, innovation, and intent.

3.11 Reflection Questions and Exercises

The development of competitive intelligence (CI) capabilities is a dynamic process that requires ongoing assessment and refinement. The following reflective questions and exercises are designed to help readers evaluate their organization's CI practices, enhance personal and team situation awareness, and implement a CI framework tailored to their business's unique context.

3.11.1 Assessing Current CI Capabilities

Reflective Questions

- How effectively does our current CI process capture changes in the external environment?
- What mechanisms are in place for analyzing and disseminating competitive insights within the organization?
- To what extent are CI insights integrated into our strategic planning and decision-making processes?

Exercise - CI Audit

Conduct an audit of your current CI processes. Identify sources of intelligence, methods of analysis, and how insights are shared and applied. Highlight areas of strength and opportunities for improvement.

3.11.2 Enhancing Personal Situation Awareness

Reflective Questions

- How regularly do I engage with external sources of information (industry reports, market analysis, news) to enhance my understanding of the competitive landscape?
- What practices do I have in place to systematically monitor competitors and market trends?

Exercise - Awareness Journal

Keep an awareness journal for a month. Each day, note down one new piece of information about competitors, market trends, or customer preferences. At the month's end, review the journal to identify patterns or insights that may have been overlooked.

3.11.3 Fostering a Collaborative Environment for Sharing Insights

Reflective Questions

- How open and effective is the communication within our team regarding competitive insights?
- Are there barriers that hinder the sharing of information and collaboration on CI?

Exercise - Insight Sharing Workshop

Organize a workshop where team members present one interesting piece of competitive intelligence they've discovered. Discuss the potential implications of these insights and explore collaborative strategies to address them.

3.11.4 Implementing a CI Framework

Reflective Questions

- Does our CI framework align with the specific needs and strategic goals of our business?
- How agile and responsive is our CI framework to changes in the external environment?

Exercise - CI Framework Design

Design a CI framework that addresses the unique aspects of your business. Define the objectives, scope, intelligence-gathering methods, analysis techniques, and dissemination processes. Ensure the framework includes mechanisms for regular review and adaptation.

Strategy Implementation Plan

Create a detailed plan for implementing the newly designed CI framework. Assign roles and responsibilities, set timelines, and determine metrics for measuring the effectiveness of the CI activities.

By engaging with these reflective questions and exercises, organizations can gain a deeper understanding of their competitive intelligence capabilities and identify practical steps for enhancement. The goal is to build a CI process that is not only robust and comprehensive but also flexible enough to adapt to the ever-changing business landscape, ensuring that the organization remains proactive and competitive.

4. Evaluate Your Position

4.1 Introduction

The imperative to continuously adapt and grow has never been more pronounced. Chapter Four delves into the crucial role of evaluating your position in the process of redesigning business models for sustainable growth. This exploration is not just about incremental changes but a dynamic reimagining of how a company creates, delivers, and captures value. It's an undertaking that requires a deep dive into the core components of the current business model, a rigorous examination of its strengths and weaknesses, and a keen understanding of the external environment.

This evaluation serves as the foundation for this transformative process. By systematically evaluating both the internal workings of the business and the external forces shaping the market, companies can identify precise areas for innovation and improvement. This chapter sets the groundwork for such a strategic overhaul, guiding businesses through the essential steps of dissecting their existing business model and conducting a comprehensive SWOT (Strengths, Weaknesses, Opportunities, Threats) analysis. This dual focus ensures that redesign efforts are both informed and targeted, maximizing the potential for growth and competitiveness.

Looking ahead, we introduce the Four Actions Framework, a powerful tool that will be explored in detail in the next chapter. This framework provides a structured approach to business model redesign, encouraging companies to systematically evaluate which aspects of their current model should be eliminated, reduced, raised, or created to unlock new value. The upcoming discussion on this framework is designed to equip businesses with a strategic lens through which they can view their operations and market potential anew.

As we navigate through this chapter, keep in mind that redesigning a business model is a dynamic process that extends beyond mere adjustment to a proactive, strategic evolution. It's about positioning your business to capitalize on new opportunities and navigate challenges with agility and insight. By laying the strategic groundwork now, we prepare to embark on a journey of innovation and growth that is both responsive to the changing business environment and anticipative of future trends.

4.2 Dissecting the Business Model

The journey towards business model redesign begins with a comprehensive dissection of the existing model. This process involves breaking down the model into its core components to understand how the company currently creates, delivers, and captures value. This section guides businesses through analysing each aspect of their business model, from their value proposition to customer relationships and revenue streams, to identify inherent strengths and potential weaknesses.

4.2.1 Customer Segments

Who are our primary customers, and what are their defining characteristics? Reflect on whether you have clearly identified all relevant segments and understand their specific needs, preferences, and purchasing behaviors. Consider if there are potential segments you may have overlooked or misunderstood.

4.2.2 Value Proposition

What unique benefits does our product or service offer to customers? Consider the specific problems you solve or the needs you meet. Evaluate how well your value proposition differentiates you from competitors and resonates with your target customers.

4.2.3 Channels

How do we reach our customers, and are these channels effective and efficient? Assess the pathways through which you communicate with and deliver value to your customers. Consider the integration of these channels and whether they align with the preferences of your customer segments.

4.2.4 Customer Relationships

What type of relationships do we maintain with our customers, and how do they align with their expectations? Think about the mechanisms you have in place for customer feedback, support, and engagement. Evaluate if these efforts effectively contribute to customer satisfaction and loyalty.

4.2.5 Revenue Streams

How does our business earn revenue, and how sustainable are these sources? Analyse the diversity and reliability of your revenue streams. Consider whether your pricing strategy maximizes profitability while still appealing to your target market.

4.2.6 Key Resources

What critical assets underpin our business model, and are they being utilized effectively? Identify the physical, intellectual, human, and financial resources crucial to delivering your value proposition. Assess if these resources provide a competitive advantage and if they are managed efficiently.

4.2.7 Key Activities

What essential actions does our business undertake to operate successfully? Reflect on the core activities that drive your business model, such as production, marketing, or sales. Consider the efficiency of these activities and their alignment with your overall strategy.

4.2.8 Key Partnerships

Who are our key partners or suppliers, and how do they contribute to our value proposition? Evaluate the strategic importance of your partnerships and supply chain relationships. Consider if these partnerships enhance your competitive positioning and if there are potential partnerships that could offer additional value.

4.2.9 Cost Structure

What are the major costs associated with our business model, and how do they impact our profitability? Break down your cost structure to understand fixed versus variable costs and the major drivers of expenses. Reflect on opportunities for cost optimization without sacrificing quality or customer satisfaction.

Approaching your business model with these questions encourages a comprehensive analysis that can uncover areas for improvement, innovation, and strategic adjustment. This reflective process is foundational for businesses aiming to redesign their model for growth, ensuring that decisions are informed by a deep understanding of both internal operations and the external competitive landscape.

4.3 Identifying Strengths and Weaknesses

Through the analysis of these components, businesses can start to identify where their current model excels and where it may fall short. Strengths are those elements that give the company a competitive edge, such as a unique value proposition, strong customer relationships, or efficient key activities. Weaknesses, on the other hand, might include underutilized channels, misaligned customer segments, or unsustainable cost structures.

This deep dive into the business model not only highlights areas for immediate improvement but also sets the stage for a more strategic redesign. By understanding the intricacies of how the business operates and generates value, companies can make informed decisions about where to innovate, streamline, or pivot their strategies for growth.

4.4 Identifying Opportunities and Threats

Incorporating competitive intelligence into the SWOT analysis enriches the strategic planning process by providing a deep dive into the external factors that influence each building block of the business model. This section outlines how to systematically explore external opportunities and threats across market trends, competitor strategies, emerging technologies, and PEST factors, emphasizing their impact on innovation, differentiation, and risk mitigation.

4.4.1 Market Trends

Opportunities: Identify shifting market trends that could open new avenues for your business model's value proposition, customer segments, or revenue streams. How can these trends enhance your business model's relevance or lead to the creation of new market niches?

Threats: Be aware of market trends that might negatively impact your business model, such as a decline in demand for certain offerings or shifts in consumer preferences. How might these trends challenge your current customer segments or value proposition?

4.4.2 Competitor Strategies

Opportunities: Analyse competitors' strategies to uncover gaps in the market or areas of unmet customer needs that your business model could capitalize on. Could adaptations to your channels or customer relationships provide a competitive edge?

Threats: Understand the strategic moves of your competitors, especially those that directly compete with your key activities or partnerships. Are competitors adopting new technologies or business models that could disrupt your market position?

4.4.3 Emerging Technologies

Opportunities: Explore how emerging technologies could be integrated into your business model to enhance your offerings, streamline operations, or create new revenue streams. Could these technologies enable you to serve your customer segments more effectively or efficiently?

Threats: Stay vigilant about technological advancements that could render aspects of your business model obsolete. How might you adapt your key resources or activities to mitigate these risks?

4.4.4 PEST Factors

Opportunities: Examine the political, economic, social, and technological environment for factors that could be leveraged to strengthen your business model. This might include regulatory changes that open up new markets or social trends that align with your value proposition.

Threats: Identify PEST factors that pose risks to your business model's viability, such as economic downturns affecting customer purchasing power or regulatory changes impacting your operations. How can your business model be adapted to withstand these external pressures?

By utilizing competitive intelligence to conduct a detailed exploration of external opportunities and threats for each building block of the business model, businesses can ensure that their strategic analysis is both comprehensive and focused. This approach not only aids in identifying where the business model can be innovated or differentiated to seize external opportunities but also highlights where it may be vulnerable to external threats. The ultimate goal is to leverage this analysis to inform a strategic redesign of the business model, positioning the company for sustained growth and competitiveness in a dynamic market landscape.

The next steps involve taking these internal insights and mapping them against the external environment through a SWOT analysis. This approach allows businesses to position their inherent strengths and identified weaknesses in the context of broader market opportunities and threats, laying a solid foundation for strategic evolution and competitive advantage.

4.5 Detailed SWOT Analysis of Business Model Building Blocks

Incorporating a detailed SWOT analysis for each building block of the Business Model Canvas, as outlined by Osterwalder and Pigneur, provides a granular approach to understanding the strategic posture of a business. This method involves dissecting the nine building blocks of the Business Model Canvas—Customer Segments, Value Propositions, Channels, Customer Relationships, Revenue Streams, Key Resources, Key Activities, Key Partnerships, and Cost Structure—through the lens of SWOT analysis. This refined approach enables businesses to identify leverage points for growth, areas of vulnerability within each segment of their business model, and align these insights with external opportunities and threats.

4.5.1 Customer Segments

Strengths: Which segments are most loyal or profitable?

Weaknesses: Are there segments being underserved or overlooked?

Opportunities: Is there an emerging customer segment your business could target?

Threats: Are there external factors affecting the purchasing power or preferences of your key segments?

4.5.2 Value Propositions

Strengths: What unique solutions do you offer to customer problems or needs?

Weaknesses: Are there gaps in your value proposition that competitors are exploiting?

Opportunities: Can trends or technologies enable new value propositions?

Threats: What changes in customer expectations or competitor offerings could undermine your value proposition?

4.5.3 Channels

Strengths: Which channels most effectively reach your customers?

Weaknesses: Are there inefficiencies or bottlenecks in your distribution channels?

Opportunities: Could new channels (e.g., digital platforms) enhance or diversify your reach?

Threats: Are there emerging risks in your distribution channels (e.g., regulatory changes, channel conflict)?

4.5.4 Customer Relationships

Strengths: What aspects of your customer service create loyalty and retention?

Weaknesses: Where are there shortcomings in customer satisfaction?

Opportunities: How can feedback or data analytics improve customer relationships?

Threats: What external factors (e.g., social media criticism) could damage customer relationships?

4.5.5 Revenue Streams

Strengths: What are the most stable and growing sources of revenue?

Weaknesses: Are there revenue streams that are underperforming or declining?

Opportunities: Is there potential for new revenue models (e.g., subscription-based, freemium)?

Threats: How could changes in market demand or competitor pricing strategies affect your revenue?

4.5.6 Key Resources

Strengths: What unique resources (e.g., intellectual property, talent) do you possess?

Weaknesses: Are there critical resource gaps or dependencies?

Opportunities: Can partnerships or investments secure new resources?

Threats: Are there risks to your key resources (e.g., talent scarcity, resource depletion)?

4.5.7 Key Activities

Strengths: Which activities drive competitive advantage (e.g., innovation, operational efficiency)?

Weaknesses: Where are there inefficiencies or areas needing improvement?

Opportunities: Could process improvements or new technologies enhance key activities?

Threats: What external changes could disrupt your operational activities?

4.5.8 Key Partnerships

Strengths: Which partnerships contribute significantly to your business model?

Weaknesses: Are there partnerships that are not delivering expected value?

Opportunities: Are there potential collaborations that could strengthen your business model?

Threats: Could changes in partner strategies or market conditions impact your partnerships?

4.5.9 Cost Structure

Strengths: Where are you achieving cost efficiencies or economies of scale?

Weaknesses: Are there areas of high cost that reduce profitability?

Opportunities: Could technological advancements or process optimizations reduce costs?

Threats: Are there upcoming changes that could increase operational costs?

By conducting a detailed SWOT analysis for each building block, businesses can create a nuanced strategic framework that not only highlights areas for immediate improvement but also identifies strategic opportunities for growth and innovation. This deep dive facilitates a holistic view of how internal capabilities and external factors intersect, enabling businesses to redesign their business model in a way that is both responsive to the current market landscape and anticipative of future trends and challenges.

4.6   Laying the Groundwork for Redesign

The journey toward business model redesign is both strategic and iterative, requiring a synthesis of internal strengths and external opportunities, alongside a vigilant approach to mitigating weaknesses and threats. This section lays the foundational strategies for leveraging competitive intelligence and SWOT analysis insights, setting the stage for a dynamic, growth-oriented business model redesign.

4.6.1   Strategic Synthesis for Growth

Leveraging Strengths and Opportunities

Begin by mapping your business's internal strengths to external opportunities. This involves identifying how your unique capabilities, resources, or market position can be aligned with emerging trends, market demands, or technological advancements to capture new growth avenues.

Consider forming strategic alliances or partnerships that amplify your strengths and directly tap into identified opportunities. This could mean collaborating with technology providers, distribution channels, or complementary service providers to create new value propositions or expand market reach.

Addressing Weaknesses and External Threats

Develop targeted strategies to address internal weaknesses that could exacerbate external threats. This might involve investing in technology to close capability gaps, restructuring operations for efficiency, or enhancing product offerings to better meet customer needs.

Prepare for potential external threats by creating contingency plans that consider the worst-case scenarios. This proactive approach ensures that the business remains resilient and can navigate challenges without significant disruption.

4.6.2   Preparing for Dynamic Redesign

The Concept of Dynamic Business Model Redesign

You must embrace the concept of business model redesign as an ongoing, responsive process. In a rapidly changing business environment, the ability to adapt and evolve continuously is crucial for long-term sustainability and growth.

Incorporate mechanisms for regular feedback, learning, and iteration within the redesign process. This could involve customer feedback channels, market testing, or performance analytics to refine and adjust the business model based on real-world insights.

Setting the Stage for the Four Actions Framework

The Four Actions Framework is a cornerstone in the realm of strategic business model redesign, offering a structured, systematic approach to scrutinizing and reconfiguring the existing business model (Kim and Mauborgne, 2005, 2017, Osterwalder and Pigneur, 2010). This methodology, rooted in the principles of innovation and strategic realignment, challenges businesses to critically evaluate their current operations through four transformative actions: Eliminate, Reduce, Raise, and Create.

This framework's power lies in its ability to guide companies in reimagining their business model components to better align with strategic objectives and capitalize on market opportunities. By applying these four actions, businesses can shift from a traditional competitive landscape to blue oceans of uncontested market space, where innovation and value creation drive growth and differentiation.

In the next chapter, we will dive deeper into the practical application of the Four Actions Framework to the business model canvas, a visual chart with elements describing a firm's value proposition, infrastructure, customers, and finances. This process involves a critical and creative examination of each component through the lens of the four actions, facilitating a comprehensive redesign of the business model.

1.   **Eliminate:** We will explore how to identify and remove elements of the business model that have become obsolete or no longer contribute to the company's goals or meet market needs. This action encourages businesses to challenge industry norms and question long-held practices that may be limiting innovation or growth.

2. **Reduce:** This step involves pinpointing aspects of the business model that can be scaled back or minimized to optimize resources and operations. By reducing complexity, companies can streamline processes, lower costs, and increase efficiency, enhancing overall competitiveness.

3. **Raise:** Here, we will focus on areas within the business model where increased investment can significantly enhance value for customers and stakeholders. This could involve improving product features, enhancing service quality, or investing in customer experience, driving greater satisfaction and loyalty.

4. **Create:** Finally, the framework prompts businesses to identify opportunities for introducing entirely new offerings or business practices. This action is about innovation and differentiation, looking beyond the current market and competitive landscape to envision new value propositions, revenue streams, or customer segments.

The forthcoming chapter promises a detailed guide to applying the Four Actions Framework, equipping businesses with the strategic insights and tools necessary for a dynamic, growth-oriented business model redesign. By methodically evaluating and adjusting each component of the business model, companies can position themselves to seize new opportunities, address challenges, and navigate the complexities of today's ever-evolving business environment.

4.7 Conclusion

As we conclude Chapter Four, we underscore the pivotal role of comprehensive strategic analysis in laying the groundwork for a successful business model redesign. This chapter has illuminated the pathway for businesses to dissect their current operations, evaluate their competitive standing, and prepare for a strategic overhaul that aligns with both internal capabilities and external market demands. The integration of strategic analysis into the fabric of business planning is not merely a preliminary step but a continuous, vital practice that sustains dynamic growth and innovation.

We advocate for businesses to embrace strategic analysis as an intrinsic component of their growth strategies, ensuring it becomes a perpetual process rather than a static, one-off exercise. This approach enables organizations to remain agile, responsive to market changes, and ahead of competitive forces, fostering an environment where innovation thrives.

4.8   Reflection Questions and Exercises

4.8.1   Reflective Questions

- What are the core strengths of your current business model, and how do they align with the identified market opportunities?
- Where are the critical weaknesses in your business model, and how do they expose your business to external threats?
- Given the external opportunities and threats identified, what elements of your business model would you consider for elimination, reduction, enhancement, or creation?

4.8.2   Exercises

SWOT Mapping Exercise

Create a detailed SWOT analysis for your business. Map each strength, weakness, opportunity, and threat to specific elements of your business model. This exercise will help visualize where strategic adjustments are needed most urgently.

Four Actions Framework Workshop

Conduct a workshop with key stakeholders in your organization to apply the Four Actions Framework to your current business model. Use the insights from your SWOT analysis to guide discussions on what to eliminate, reduce, raise, and create. Document these sessions to capture innovative ideas and strategic insights.

Continuous Innovation Plan

Develop a plan that outlines how your business will continuously monitor the internal and external environment for cues to evolve the business model. Include mechanisms for regular strategic reviews, competitive intelligence gathering, and market analysis to ensure your business model remains aligned with changing dynamics.

By engaging with these questions and exercises, businesses can start the journey toward not only redesigning their business model but also embedding a culture of strategic agility and continuous innovation. The forthcoming application of the Four Actions Framework promises to offer a structured approach to this redesign, empowering businesses to navigate their competitive landscapes with precision and foresight. The goal is to not just adapt to changes but to anticipate and shape them, securing a sustainable path to growth and success.

5. (Re)Design for Growth

5.1 Introduction

In the preceding chapter, we laid the groundwork for a strategic overhaul by dissecting the business model and incorporating SWOT analysis to identify the strengths, weaknesses, opportunities, and threats that shape our competitive landscape. Building on this foundation, Chapter Five delves into the transformative journey of business model redesign through the application of the Four Actions Framework, a cornerstone of the Blue Ocean Strategy (Kim and Mauborgne, 2005, 2017), which provides a systematic approach to rethinking and reshaping business strategies for unmatched innovation and differentiation.

The Four Actions Framework prompts businesses to rigorously evaluate every aspect of their current operations, challenging them to eliminate outdated elements, reduce overdesigned features, raise value in key areas, and create entirely new elements that the industry has yet to offer. This chapter will explore how this powerful strategy not only streamlines existing models for efficiency and effectiveness but also propels businesses into new markets and customer segments, fostering growth and sustainability.

By encouraging a departure from the competitive battlegrounds of red oceans, the Four Actions Framework guides companies toward the creation of blue oceans — untapped new market spaces ripe for growth. The application of this framework is not just about incremental improvements but about redefining the rules of the game, offering unparalleled value to customers and securing a competitive advantage that is both unique and sustainable.

As we navigate through this chapter, we aim to inspire businesses to embrace the Four Actions Framework not merely as a tool for strategic analysis but as a beacon for innovation and growth. Through this approach, companies are equipped to transcend traditional competition, unveiling new horizons for profitability and success in the ever-evolving business landscape.

5.2 Understanding the Four Actions Framework

5.2.1 Overview

The Four Actions Framework is a strategic tool designed to systematically reassess and innovate a company's business model. It consists of four key actions — Eliminate, Reduce, Raise, and Create — which guide businesses in rethinking their strategies to break free from traditional competitive battles and venture into new market spaces, or "blue oceans." This framework is instrumental in pushing companies to not only scrutinize their current operations but also to envision and implement changes that drive significant value innovation.

At its core, the Four Actions Framework challenges businesses to ask four fundamental questions:

1. What factors that the industry takes for granted can be eliminated?
2. Which factors should be reduced well below the industry's standard?
3. What factors should be raised well above the industry's standard?
4. Which factors should be created that the industry has never offered?

By answering these questions, businesses can reconstruct market boundaries, focus on the big picture, reach beyond existing demand, and ensure the strategic sequence of their moves. The ultimate goal is to create new value for customers and the company, thereby opening up new and uncontested market space.

5.2.2 Historical Context and Evolution

Developed by W. Chan Kim and Renée Mauborgne, the Four Actions Framework was introduced as a central element of Blue Ocean Strategy, first published in 2005 (Kim and Mauborgne, 2005) and later expanded in 2017 (Kim and Mauborgne, 2017). Blue Ocean Strategy challenges the traditional competitive strategy's focus on battling competitors in "red oceans," where industries are crowded, and the market space is well defined and exploited. Instead, it advocates for creating "blue oceans" of uncontested market space, ripe for growth.

The origins of the framework lie in a comprehensive study of 150 strategic moves spanning more than 100 years and 30 industries. Kim and Mauborgne (2005) identified that lasting success often comes not from battling competitors but from creating blue oceans of new market space. The Four Actions Framework emerged as a practical tool to help businesses systematically achieve this shift.

Over the years, the framework has been successfully applied across a diverse range of industries, from automotive to healthcare, and from consumer goods to technology. Companies that have embraced the framework have not only differentiated themselves from competitors but have also established new standards and expectations within their industries. These success stories underscore the framework's versatility and its potential to drive innovation and growth in any business context.

In essence, the Four Actions Framework provides a clear and actionable roadmap for companies seeking to transcend traditional competitive strategies and explore new horizons of opportunity and growth. Through its systematic approach to innovation and differentiation, the framework empowers businesses to redefine their industries and create their own blue oceans.

5.3   Applying the Framework to Business Model Redesign

The Four Actions Framework serves as a transformative tool in the redesign of business models, guiding companies through the process of systematically re-evaluating and reconstructing their approach to the market. Here's how businesses can apply each action of the framework to innovate and grow.

5.3.1   Eliminate

Conduct a thorough analysis of your business model to pinpoint outdated or redundant elements. This can involve evaluating customer feedback, industry trends, and competitive benchmarks to identify what no longer serves your market effectively.

Challenge the status quo by questioning the necessity of long-standing industry practices. Often, elements that are considered industry standards can be eliminated without detracting from customer value.

For example, many businesses find that traditional forms of marketing or sales channels, like print advertising or brick-and-mortar stores, can be eliminated in favour of digital platforms which offer greater reach and efficiency. A further example is eliminating complex and rarely used features from products or services that complicate the customer experience without adding significant value.

5.3.2 Reduce

Identify areas of your business model that are overdesigned or where resources are being used inefficiently. This involves a critical look at your product features, services, and customer support processes to determine what exceeds customer needs.

Implement lean principles to streamline operations and reduce waste, focusing on simplifying products and processes while maintaining the essence of what customers truly value.

A software company might reduce its application's complexity by removing seldom-used features that confuse users, focusing instead on streamlining the user interface for a better customer experience.

Retail businesses could scale back their product lines to focus on high-demand items, reducing inventory costs and simplifying supply chain management.

5.3.3 Raise

Through customer feedback and market analysis, identify aspects of your business model where increasing investment can significantly enhance customer satisfaction and loyalty. This might involve improving product quality, customer service responsiveness, or adding value-added services.

Look for opportunities to go above and beyond industry norms, providing customers with an experience or product quality that sets your business apart.

A hotel chain might raise its level of customer service by introducing personalized guest experiences, leveraging this enhancement for better positioning in the luxury segment and justifying premium pricing.

A tech company could invest in superior after-sales support, significantly increasing customer satisfaction and fostering brand loyalty in a competitive market.

5.3.4 Create

Identify gaps in the market where customer needs are still unmet or emerging trends offer new opportunities. This requires a deep understanding of your customers and a forward-looking view of the industry.

Engage in creative brainstorming sessions, encouraging bold ideas and outside-the-box thinking to conceive new products, services, or business models that the industry has not yet seen, for example:

Potential for Market Redefinition:

- The introduction of subscription-based models in traditional industries, such as automotive or appliances, meeting customers' desire for flexibility and ongoing service rather than outright ownership.
- The development of new technology platforms that connect disparate services in a seamless ecosystem, offering convenience and added value that redefines consumer expectations and creates new market space.

By applying the Four Actions Framework to their business model redesign, companies can embark on a strategic overhaul that not only refines and streamlines their existing operations but also propels them into new territories of growth and innovation. This approach encourages businesses to break free from the competitive deadlock and venture into blue oceans of uncontested market space, where differentiation and value innovation drive sustainable profitability.

5.4   The Strategic Overhaul Process

The journey from the evaluation of a current business model to the strategic implementation of a redesigned model is both complex and rewarding. Applying the Four Actions Framework effectively requires a disciplined approach, navigating from conceptual analysis through to tangible changes in the business structure and market approach. This section outlines the steps in this process, highlights transformational case studies, and discusses potential challenges and strategic considerations.

5.4.1   From Evaluation to Implementation

Initial Analysis

Begin with a comprehensive analysis of the existing business model, focusing on understanding how each component delivers value to customers and contributes to the business's success. This should include gathering extensive customer feedback, competitive intelligence, and market analysis.

Application of the Four Actions Framework

Systematically apply the Eliminate, Reduce, Raise, and Create actions to each aspect of the business model. This involves challenging every assumption, seeking areas for simplification, and identifying opportunities for innovation.

Business Model (Re)design

Based on insights gained from the Four Actions Framework, develop a business model design that outlines new business model components, including revised value propositions, customer segments, revenue models, and operational processes.

Implementation

Roll out the redesigned business model, starting with pilot projects or in phases to test and refine the changes. Ensure that there is a robust system for monitoring performance and gathering feedback for continuous improvement.

Continuous Evaluation

Establish mechanisms for ongoing evaluation and adaptation of the business model, ensuring it remains responsive to customer needs, market dynamics, and competitive pressures.

5.4.2 Case Studies of Transformation

Cirque du Soleil

By eliminating expensive star performers and animal shows (Eliminate), reducing the emphasis on traditional circus elements (Reduce), raising the level of artistry and storyline (Raise), and creating a unique fusion of theatre and circus (Create), Cirque du Soleil successfully entered a blue ocean, redefining the entertainment industry.

Netflix

Transitioning from a DVD rental service to a streaming platform, Netflix phased out physical media (Eliminate), streamlined its content acquisition strategy (Reduce), invested heavily in original content (Raise), and introduced a subscription-based streaming model (Create), transforming the way people consume media and entering new global markets.

5.4.3 Challenges and Considerations

Resistance to Change

One of the primary challenges is overcoming internal resistance, whether due to cultural inertia or fear of the unknown. Leadership must foster a culture that values innovation and is open to change.

Market Misalignment

There is always a risk that the redesigned business model may not align perfectly with market needs or expectations. Continuous market testing and customer feedback are crucial to mitigating this risk.

Resource Constraints

Particularly for smaller businesses or those in highly competitive industries, there may be significant constraints on the resources available to implement a comprehensive redesign. Strategic prioritization and phased implementation can help manage these constraints.

Adapting to Growth Stages

The application of the Four Actions Framework must be tailored to the business's stage of growth, with start-ups possibly focusing more on creation and innovation, while established companies might emphasize eliminating inefficiencies and raising value in their offerings.

By navigating these steps and considerations, businesses can embark on a strategic overhaul that not only enhances their current operations but also positions them for growth in new markets and sectors. The Four Actions Framework offers a structured pathway to rethink and innovate business models, driving sustainable success in an ever-evolving competitive landscape.

5.5 Conclusion

The exploration of the Four Actions Framework within this chapter underscores its profound capability to catalyse business model redesign and foster market differentiation. This strategic tool is not merely about tweaking existing elements for marginal improvements; it represents a comprehensive overhaul that challenges businesses to eliminate the obsolete, reduce the superfluous, raise standards where it matters most, and create ground-breaking innovations. Its application is a testament to the framework's potential to drive businesses beyond the confines of competitive battlegrounds and into the expansive realms of blue oceans — markets untapped and undefined by the current industry parameters.

We extend a call to action for businesses across the spectrum — from start-ups to established giants, from service providers to product developers, but especially mid-career entrepreneurs — to harness the power of this strategic overhaul. By adopting the Four Actions Framework, businesses commit not just to incremental enhancements but to radical innovation and the creation of new market spaces. This journey demands a departure from conventional strategies, urging a pivot towards reimagining how value is delivered and perceived by customers.

5.6 Reflection Questions and Exercises

5.6.1 Reflective Questions

- Which aspects of your current business model could be considered for elimination due to their lack of value addition to your customers or your bottom line?
- Are there elements within your operations or offerings that could be reduced to streamline processes and better align with customer priorities?
- What features, services, or customer touchpoints can be raised to exceed industry standards and significantly enhance customer satisfaction?
- Where do you see opportunities for creating new elements within your business model that could address unmet customer needs or capitalize on emerging market trends?

5.6.2 Exercises

Four Actions Workshop

Organize a workshop with your team to apply the Four Actions Framework to your current business model. Use the reflective questions as a guide to facilitate discussion and ideation.

Customer Feedback Integration

Design a survey or feedback mechanism to gather insights from your customers about potential areas for elimination, reduction, enhancement, or innovation. Use this feedback to inform your application of the framework.

Market Trends Analysis

Conduct a comprehensive analysis of emerging trends within your industry and broader market. Map these trends against the Four Actions to identify where new opportunities for creation might lie.

This chapter aims to equip businesses with a robust and dynamic strategy for growth, leveraging the transformative potential of the Four Actions Framework. By guiding companies through the process of critically assessing and innovating their business models, it paves the way for uncharted territories of market innovation and unparalleled customer value. Embracing this framework is embracing a future where continuous innovation and strategic agility are not just ideals but integral components of everyday business practice.

6. Manage Your Life

6.1 Introduction

In Chapter 6, we embark on a transformative journey towards designing a life where personal fulfillment and professional success are not just parallel tracks but deeply intertwined paths. This chapter isn't about choosing between a thriving career and a fulfilling personal life; it's about creating a harmonious blend where each aspect enriches the other, leading to a more holistic sense of wealth and well-being.

Our exploration is enriched by the collaboration with our strategic partners at *Design a Decade*, experts in crafting strategies that transcend traditional financial planning (Freeman, 2016). Together, we delve into the art and science of building wealth in its most comprehensive sense. This isn't about pinpointing the next lucrative real estate investment or hot stock tip. Instead, we focus on cultivating a lifestyle that systematically fosters both financial prosperity and day-to-day joy, setting the foundation for a life well-lived long before the conventional retirement age.

This chapter is dedicated to unveiling how you can safely and progressively construct a life rich in experiences, relationships, and personal achievement, all while building financial stability. We dissect:

- Effective time management strategies that apply to all areas of life, ensuring that your days contribute to long-term goals without sacrificing the present.
- The cultivation of trusted personal and professional relationships that support and enhance your journey.
- The implementation of simple yet effective systems for managing income and expenditure, providing clarity and control over your financial landscape.
- Comprehensive planning techniques that encompass all life domains, empowering you to critically assess advice and make informed decisions.
- Processes designed to sustain your energy and vitality, enabling you to embrace the journey of life with enthusiasm and resilience.
- Methodical approaches to accumulating financial wealth in an orderly, progressive manner, tailored to your unique life vision.

By the end of this chapter, you will be equipped with the insights and tools necessary to design a life that not only meets but exceeds your aspirations. This is about laying a foundation for a lifestyle where work and personal fulfillment are not at odds but are components of a grander vision for wealth and well-being. Read on as we redefine what it means to live well, challenging the norms and setting new standards for success and happiness.

6.2 Foundations of a Well-Integrated Life

Creating a life that harmoniously blends personal fulfillment with professional success starts with a solid foundation in two critical areas: True Time Management and Cultivating Trusted Relationships. These elements are essential in navigating the complexities of modern life, ensuring that every aspect, from career to leisure, contributes to a holistic sense of wealth and well-being.

6.2.1 True Time Management

Strategies for Managing Time Effectively Across All Life Areas

Time is a finite resource, making its management crucial for achieving a well-integrated life. Effective time management goes beyond mere scheduling; it's about aligning your daily actions with your ultimate life and career aspirations. Strategies include:

- **Life Auditing**: Periodically review how you spend your time across various life domains — work, personal growth, leisure — to ensure balance. Identify areas where time is not being used effectively or in alignment with your goals.
- **Goal-Oriented Planning**: Set clear, actionable goals for different aspects of your life. Use these goals to guide how you allocate your time, ensuring that each day moves you closer to your desired outcomes.

Techniques for Prioritizing Tasks and Commitments

The Eisenhower Matrix: Utilize this tool to categorize tasks based on their urgency and importance, helping to focus on what truly matters and avoid spending time on low-priority activities.

Time Blocking: Dedicate specific blocks of time to different activities or goals. This technique helps in maintaining focus and ensuring dedicated time for work, personal development, and relaxation.

Cultivating Trusted Relationships

Relationships are the bedrock of a fulfilled life and a successful career. They provide support, inspiration, and opportunities for growth. Emphasizing the cultivation of deep, meaningful connections can enrich your journey in immeasurable ways, for example:

- **Mutual Growth**: Seek relationships that offer mutual support and opportunities for growth. Surrounding yourself with individuals who inspire you and whom you can inspire in return creates a network of empowerment.
- **Trust and Respect**: Foundations of any lasting relationship. Investing time in understanding others, showing empathy, and being reliable builds trust and mutual respect, essential for both personal and professional connections.

Guidance on Building and Maintaining a Network of Trust and Mutual Respect

Consistent Communication: Regularly engage with your network through various means — whether through social media, networking events, or personal meetups. Consistency in communication keeps relationships strong and active.

Give and Take: Relationships thrive on reciprocity. Be ready to offer your support, knowledge, and time to others. Likewise, be open to receiving help, advice, and mentorship. This balance of give and take fosters a network of trust and mutual respect.

By laying these foundations, you set the stage for a life where time is not just spent but invested wisely, and relationships are not merely formed but nurtured deeply. These practices enable the construction of a life well-integrated with work, filled with growth, satisfaction, and meaningful connections, setting a solid groundwork for further development in financial stability and lifestyle wealth.

6.3   Financial and Lifestyle Wealth Building

Achieving a well-integrated life extends into the realm of financial stability and prosperity. This section delves into practical strategies for managing income and expenditures and outlines a systematic approach to wealth building that aligns with your broader life goals. It's about creating a financial foundation that supports not just your immediate needs but also your long-term aspirations for a rich and fulfilling life.

6.3.1 Managing Income and Expenditure

Establishing a robust system for managing personal finances is crucial. This starts with the basics of budgeting, where you track income and expenses to understand where your money is going. Budgeting creates a clear picture of your financial health, allowing you to make adjustments where necessary.

Saving is another pillar of financial stability. Setting aside a portion of your income regularly builds a safety net for unforeseen expenses and future investments. Techniques like automating your savings can make this process effortless and consistent.

Investing is where you can turn savings into wealth. Understanding the basics of investing, from the stock market to real estate, is essential. Starting with low-risk investments and gradually expanding your portfolio can help grow your wealth over time.

Educate yourself on financial products and investment vehicles. Knowledge is power when it comes to making informed decisions that affect your financial future.

Consider consulting with a financial advisor to tailor a financial plan that suits your specific life and career goals. They can provide insights into opportunities you might not have considered and help you avoid common pitfalls.

6.3.2 Systematic Wealth Building

Building wealth is a marathon, not a sprint. Developing a long-term investment strategy that reflects your risk tolerance and life goals is vital. This might involve a mix of stocks, bonds, real estate, and other assets to provide both growth and security.

Avoid the allure of get-rich-quick schemes (e.g., cryptocurrencies). Sustainable wealth building is about making consistent, calculated investment choices that compound over time.

Diversification is key to reducing risk in your investment portfolio. By spreading investments across different asset classes and sectors, you can buffer against market volatility and protect your wealth in fluctuating economic conditions.

Consider both traditional and alternative investments. While stocks and bonds are considered foundational by some, real estate is key to securing your future. Alternative investments like commodities, or even art can offer unique opportunities for growth and diversification.

By adopting a disciplined approach to managing income and expenditure and strategically building wealth, you can create a financial foundation that supports a life of personal and professional fulfillment. This systematic approach to financial and lifestyle wealth building ensures that you're not just working towards retirement but crafting a life that is rich in experiences, achievements, and satisfaction at every stage.

6.4 Holistic Life Planning

Embarking on a journey towards a well-integrated life necessitates a holistic approach to planning that encompasses all facets of existence. This section delves into the methodologies for comprehensive life planning and the importance of self-education in making informed decisions. Additionally, it explores the crucial aspect of maintaining energy and freshness, ensuring sustained vitality and enthusiasm throughout life's myriad phases.

6.4.1 Comprehensive Life Planning

Holistic life planning involves taking a broad view of your life, considering career ambitions, financial goals, health and wellness, personal development, and relationships. Begin by setting clear, actionable goals in each of these areas, ensuring they are interrelated and support one another.

Employ visualization techniques and tools like vision boards or life maps to articulate and organize your goals. This can help in identifying priorities and the steps needed to achieve them.

Regular review sessions are crucial for assessing progress and making necessary adjustments. Life is dynamic; as such, your plan should be flexible, allowing for shifts in priorities and strategies.

Equip yourself with knowledge across different domains of life planning. This doesn't mean becoming an expert in every field but understanding enough to evaluate advice critically and make decisions that align with your values and circumstances.

Leverage resources like books, online courses, workshops, and mentorships to broaden your understanding. Diverse perspectives can enrich your knowledge base and open new possibilities.

Learn to question and seek clarity when receiving advice from professionals, whether financial advisors, career coaches, or health experts. This ensures that the guidance you follow is truly in your best interest.

6.4.2 Maintaining Energy and Freshness

The foundation of maintaining energy and freshness lies in a balanced lifestyle that prioritizes physical health, mental well-being, and emotional resilience. Incorporate regular physical activity, balanced nutrition, and sufficient rest into your daily routine.

Mindfulness practices, such as meditation and yoga, can significantly enhance mental clarity and emotional stability. They help in managing stress, fostering a sense of inner peace, and improving focus and productivity.

Continuous learning and personal development are not just avenues for career advancement but are also vital for maintaining intellectual curiosity and emotional vitality. Challenge yourself to step out of your comfort zone, whether by learning a new skill, exploring a new hobby, or engaging in new experiences.

Recognize self-care as an essential component of your holistic life plan, not a luxury. This means setting aside time for activities that rejuvenate your mind, body, and soul.

Cultivate habits that support sustained energy levels and prevent burnout. This could include setting boundaries to protect your time, practicing gratitude, and ensuring leisure and social activities are part of your routine.

Embrace the concept of "rest as productive" to allow for periods of downtime that facilitate creativity, problem-solving, and overall well-being.

By adopting a holistic approach to life planning and emphasizing the importance of maintaining energy and freshness, you pave the way for a life that is not only successful on the outside but also deeply fulfilling and vibrant from within. This comprehensive strategy ensures that you are well-prepared to navigate the complexities of life, making informed decisions that resonate with your personal values and long-term aspirations.

6.5 Risk Mitigation and Long-Term Security

In the pursuit of designing a life well-integrated with work and personal fulfillment, mitigating risks and ensuring long-term security are paramount. This section explores strategies to minimize potential mistakes in personal and financial decision-making and outlines approaches to achieve life success well before the traditional retirement age.

6.5.1   Reducing the Risk of Mistakes

Strategies for minimizing potential errors include:

- **Due diligence**. Before making significant decisions, especially those related to finances or career changes, conduct thorough research to understand all implications. Due diligence involves assessing the risks, benefits, and long-term impacts of your choices.
- **Continuous education**. Stay informed about trends and changes in your industry, investment opportunities, and personal development practices. An ongoing commitment to learning helps you make more informed decisions and stay ahead of potential pitfalls.
- **Seeking expert advice**. Recognize when professional guidance is needed. Whether it's a financial advisor, career coach, or therapist, consulting with experts can provide valuable insights and help you avoid common mistakes.

6.5.2   Setting Up for Early Life Success

Plan for achievements before traditional retirement age:

- **Financial independence**. Develop a financial plan that aims for independence well before the conventional retirement age. This could involve aggressive savings, strategic investments, and building passive income streams to secure your financial future early on.
- **Personal fulfillment**. Identify what personal fulfillment looks like for you, beyond the confines of your career. Whether it's pursuing hobbies, travel, or philanthropy, plan for these aspirations in your life strategy to ensure a well-rounded sense of achievement.
- **Career satisfaction**. Set career goals that align with your passions and values. Consider lateral moves, entrepreneurial ventures, or further education as paths to career satisfaction that also contribute to your broader life goals.

Creating a Flexible, Resilient Plan:

- **Anticipate changes and challenges**. Life is unpredictable. Build flexibility into your life plans to accommodate unforeseen changes, whether they're personal, professional, or financial.
- **Resilience building**. Cultivate resilience by adopting a growth mindset, practicing stress-reduction techniques, and maintaining a strong support network. Resilience is key to navigating life's ups and downs while staying on track toward your goals.

- **Regular plan evaluation**. Periodically review and adjust your life plan to reflect changes in your circumstances, aspirations, and the external environment. This iterative process ensures that your plan remains relevant and aligned with your evolving life vision.

By adopting these strategies for risk mitigation and early life success planning, you can navigate the complexities of integrating work and personal life with confidence. The goal is to not only achieve financial independence and career satisfaction but to do so in a way that fosters personal fulfillment and long-term well-being. This holistic approach to life planning empowers you to design a life that is both prosperous and profoundly satisfying, well ahead of traditional timelines.

6.6 Conclusion

Throughout this chapter, we've embarked on a comprehensive exploration of designing a life that beautifully integrates work and personal aspirations. This holistic approach underscores the significance of not merely striving for professional success or personal fulfillment in isolation but weaving them together into a rich tapestry that defines a truly enriched life. By delving into strategies for effective time management, nurturing trusted relationships, systematically building financial and lifestyle wealth, and planning for all life areas, we've laid out a roadmap for a life that transcends conventional definitions of success.

We encourage you to embrace systematic planning as a cornerstone for this journey. The meticulous design of your life's blueprint, encompassing career goals, financial stability, personal growth, and relationships, forms the pillars upon which a fulfilling life is built. Remember, wealth is not just financial; it's the abundance of time, happiness, and meaningful connections that truly enrich our lives.

6.6.1 Reflective Questions

How well does my current lifestyle integrate my professional ambitions with my personal aspirations? Where do I see imbalances or areas of neglect?

In what areas of my life could systematic planning improve my satisfaction and success? How can I begin to implement these changes?

What steps have I taken to build and maintain relationships that support my journey? Are there opportunities I'm missing to deepen these connections?

How confident do I feel in my approach to managing finances and building wealth? Where could I benefit from further education or professional advice?

6.6.2   Exercises

Time Management Audit

Spend a week tracking how you allocate your time across various activities. Reflect on how well this allocation aligns with your priorities and goals. Identify changes you can make to better balance work, personal growth, and leisure.

Financial Planning Template

Use or create a financial planning template to map out your income, expenses, savings, and investments. Set short-term and long-term financial goals, and outline strategies to achieve them. Consider areas for reducing unnecessary expenditure and opportunities for investment.

Energy Maintenance Routine

Develop a routine that incorporates practices for maintaining your physical, mental, and emotional energy. This could include exercise, meditation, hobbies, or learning new skills. Schedule these activities into your week as non-negotiable appointments with yourself.

By engaging with these reflective questions and exercises, you're taking meaningful steps toward designing a life that not only meets but surpasses your expectations. This chapter aims to inspire and equip you with the tools and strategies necessary for crafting a life marked by professional achievement, personal growth, and deep satisfaction. The journey to a well-integrated life is ongoing and ever-evolving, rich with opportunities for learning, growth, and fulfillment.

Work You Love with People You Like the Way You Want[1]

We've journeyed through the multifaceted process of designing not just a business, but a life that resonates with our deepest aspirations for success, fulfillment, and happiness. From the strategic deployment of the Four Actions Framework for business model innovation to the holistic planning for a life well-integrated with work, this book serves as a guide for those seeking to craft a reality defined by both professional achievement and personal satisfaction.

We've explored the significance of true time management, the cultivation of trusted relationships, and the systematic building of financial and lifestyle wealth as pillars upon which a fulfilling life can be constructed. By embracing the principles of the Four Actions Framework applied to your business model and its environment, we've learned how to navigate beyond the competitive battlegrounds of red oceans into the uncharted territories of blue oceans, where innovation and differentiation drive sustainable growth and profitability.

The central thesis of this book revolves around the belief that it's entirely possible to create work you love, build meaningful relationships with people you like, and live your life exactly how you want. This requires a deliberate and thoughtful approach to life and business design, where strategic planning meets personal introspection.

Your Next Best Step

Reflect on Your Current Path

Take a moment to consider where you stand today in relation to your goals for your business and your life. Are you moving towards work you love? Are you cultivating relationships with people you genuinely enjoy? Is your daily life reflective of how you want to live?

---

[1] The title of this chapter is from the work of two of my mentors and another colleague: Church, M., Cook, P. & Stein, S. 2016. *The Thought Leaders Practice*, Thought Leaders Publishing..

Conduct a Strategic Audit

Utilize the tools and strategies discussed, such as the Four Actions Framework and SWOT analysis, to evaluate your current business model and life design. Identify areas for innovation, growth, and improvement.

Plan for Holistic Wealth Building

Beyond financial success, consider what lifestyle wealth means to you. Begin to systematically plan for both financial stability and the richness of experiences, relationships, and personal fulfillment.

Implement a Time Management and Energy Maintenance Routine

Start with auditing how you spend your time and energy. Develop a routine that aligns more closely with your priorities, ensuring that you're investing in areas that bring you closer to your ideal business and life.

Cultivate and Nurture Relationships

Identify key relationships in your personal and professional life that need attention or strengthening. Take active steps to enrich these connections.

Swim Towards Your Blue Ocean

Identify one action you can take today that moves you closer to carving out your unique market space — one where you do work you love, in a way that brings you joy and satisfaction.

Conclusion

The Growth Business is more than just a book; it's a call to action for every reader to take charge of their destiny by designing their business and life with intention and purpose. What you decide to do today, no matter how small, can set you on the path to growth and fulfillment. Remember, the journey to a life and business you love is iterative and evolving. Each step you take, informed by strategic analysis and personal reflection, brings you closer to realizing your vision.

The question now is not if you can achieve work you love with people you like the way you want, but what you will do today to make that vision a reality? Let this be the moment you choose to grow your business—and your life—by design.

Work with me and unleash your design for growth

We work with mid-career entrepreneurs and business owners: individuals, probably having transitioned out of a professional role, who have successfully navigated the initial stages of entrepreneurship and are now facing the challenges of scaling their businesses. They seek to grow their business by at least 20% annually while also aiming to massively reduce their work time to enjoy life more. They have likely experienced the "feast or famine" cycle and are looking for strategies to achieve consistent revenue growth, control costs, and enhance their quality of life beyond the hustle.

Our "system"? We don't have one as such – other than what we outline in this book. Everyone is different and we draw on 40 years of working with and studying people and their behaviours. We don't do "packaged solutions" because most people's challenges are unique in one way or another.

We have a problem-solving framework, called SORTED, which give us little structure to work with (Smallman, 2023). Broadly speaking, we work with clients developing a deep understanding of their business model and the environment in which they operate, redesigning the model according to the market and competitive situation. In parallel, we redesign their life, or at least bring it under a new management approach.

There are no rules to what we do. Rather like the Pirates' Code, it's more a set of guidelines.

If you would like to know more, drop Clive a line: clive@clivesmallman.com

References

Aguilar, F. J. 1967. *Scanning the Business Environment*, Macmillan.

Church, M., Cook, P. & Stein, S. 2016. *The Thought Leaders Practice*, Thought Leaders Publishing.

Freeman, C. J. 2016. *Design a Decade: Tidy up your past. Enjoy today. Set up your future.*, Balanced Wealth Creation.

Haropoulou, M. & Smallman, C. 2019. *Decision-Making for New Product Development in Small Businesses,* Abingdon, Routledge.

Kim, W. C. & Mauborgne, R. 1997. Value innovation - the strategic logic of high growth. *Harvard Business Review, 75,* 103-112.

Kim, W. C. & Mauborgne, R. 2005. *Blue Ocean Strategy: How to Create Uncontested Market Space and Make the Competition Irrelevant,* Cambridge, MA, USA, Harvard Business School Press.

Kim, W. C. & Mauborgne, R. 2017. *Blue Ocean Shift: Beyond Competing,* Macmillan.

Osterwalder, A. & Pigneur, Y. 2010. *Business Model Generation: A Handbook for Visionaries, Game Changers, and Challengers,* Chichester, John Wiley and Sons.

Smallman, C. 2023. *Sorted: Taming Wicked Problems with Smart Leadership Thinking,* Grammar Factory.

Acknowledgements

A note of appreciation for the ongoing guidance of Chris Freeman.

Also, thanks to Robin Nickerson and Taki Moore of Million Dollar Coach.

As always thank you for everything Mary.

About the author

Drawing upon a distinguished career that spans over four decades, Emeritus Professor Clive Smallman has established himself as a vanguard in the realms of leadership, management, and business. With a foundation rooted in higher degrees in business and management learning, Clive's expertise is not just academic; it's a testament to a life dedicated to the practical application of profound business principles. As a Cambridge research fellow and later as a professor elsewhere, he has imbued his work with rigorous academic discipline, yet it's his real-world experience that truly sets him apart. Having collaborated with major brands such as GEC, Centrica, Aviva, Ford, and Coca-Cola, Clive brings a wealth of knowledge and experience to every endeavour.

As the founder and head coach of Design for Growth, Clive is passionately committed to guiding mid-career entrepreneurs and professionals through the complexities of business growth and personal fulfillment. His coaching philosophy transcends the mere mechanics of business, delving into the strategic and psychological facets of entrepreneurship. Clive is an architect of success for those transitioning from employment to entrepreneurship, especially for highly skilled university-educated individuals who seek to navigate the uncharted waters of business ownership without the traditional business training.

Clive's approach is holistic, focusing on overcoming the "feast or famine" cycle, controlling costs, reducing work hours, and enhancing life enjoyment. He believes in moving beyond the hustle, advocating for a balanced life where work serves as a platform for personal growth and fulfillment. His strategies are not about relentless pursuit but about intelligent design and strategic growth, ensuring his clients not only succeed in business but thrive in life.

Moreover, as a CEO of a higher-education startup and a director of two companies, as well as a charity addressing global challenges, Clive's leadership extends to pioneering initiatives that aim to make a significant impact beyond the business sphere. His work is driven by a deep-seated belief in the power of education, leadership, and strategic thinking to transform lives and communities.

Clive Smallman, PhD, is not just a coach or a business leader; he is a visionary who believes in the transformative power of knowledge, strategy, and purposeful action. Through his work, Clive continues to inspire and empower a new generation of leaders and entrepreneurs to achieve their fullest potential, making a lasting impact on the world of business and beyond.